Headshook

Headshook

*Contemporary novelists and poets
writing on Scotland's future*

Edited by Stuart Kelly

First published in 2009 by
HACHETTE SCOTLAND, an imprint of
HACHETTE UK

1

Cataloguing in Publication Data is available from the British Library

ISBN 978 0 7553 6000 0

Typeset by Ellipsis Books Limited, Glasgow
Printed and bound in Great Britain by Clays Ltd, St Ives plc

Hachette Scotland's policy is to use papers that are natural, renewable
and recyclable products and made from wood grown in sustainable forests.
The logging and manufacturing processes are expected to conform
to the environmental regulations of the country of origin.

HACHETTE SCOTLAND
An Hachette UK Company
338 Euston Road
London NW1 3BH

www.hachettescotland.co.uk
www.hachette.co.uk

CONTENTS

Foreword   ALEX SALMOND   vii

Introduction   STUART KELLY   1

Time Capsule   ALAN SPENCE   15

Burnswear   ROBERT CRAWFORD   25

Raised Beach   KATHLEEN JAMIE   29

Do dh'Alba   AONGHAS MACNEACAIL   33

Jellyfish   JANICE GALLOWAY   39

A humanist   TOM LEONARD   55

Foreigners   ANDREW O'HAGAN   59

Unexpected Events at Four in the Morning   RON BUTLIN   81

The Circle   DON PATERSON   95

End-Sang   W. N. HERBERT   99

Aisling   RODY GORMAN   103

Tam O'Shanter   ALASDAIR GRAY   107

Faust   ALASDAIR GRAY   111

Common   ALI SMITH   113

Through A Raised Glass   RODDY LUMSDEN   131

The Last Midgie on Earth   ANDREW CRUMEY   135

The Fair Chase   JOHN BURNSIDE   149

MacTaggart's Shed   JAMES ROBERTSON   163

talking about my wife   JAMES KELMAN   183

Not Changed   LIZ LOCHHEAD   211

Mind Away   JACKIE KAY   219

Through the Tweed   ROBIN ROBERTSON   235

Burdalane   WILLIAM MCILVANNEY   239

An Stoirm   ANNE FRATER   249

Blackthorn Winter   A. L. KENNEDY   255

Blind Billy's Pride   ALAN WARNER   267

Acknowledgements   279

FOREWORD

Alex Salmond

Welcome to this collection of new work by some of Scotland's finest writers. This *Scotland on Sunday* anthology brings together an array of talent, from our leading poets and novelists.

Scotland has always been a nation which loves argument, and this has been reflected in our literature from medieval times with works such as *The Flyting of Dunbar* and *Kennedie*. I'm sure this anthology, which looks to encourage debate around Scotland's future, will continue this tradition.

It seems particularly apt to be celebrating our contemporary writers during Scotland's year of Homecoming, marking the 250th anniversary of the birth of our greatest literary figure, Robert Burns.

There are few, if any, other poets whose life and work are celebrated so widely right around the world. He is also an international cultural icon of whom all Scots can be justifiably proud. His vast and brilliant work provides inspiration for modern Scots and many far beyond our shores. The universal and timeless appeal of his words has spoken to people all over the globe down through the years, whatever their colour, creed and beliefs.

The unique ability that Burns' words have to break down barriers and transcend borders is what makes him so special. The egalitarian ideals which run through his work are nowhere better seen than in *A Man's A Man for A' That*, which was so memorably sung at the opening of the first Scottish Parliament by Sheena Wellington.

The publication of this collection is timely as this year marks the tenth anniversary of devolution, which presents an opportunity to consider how the Parliament has influenced and affected Scottish society. I hope this book stimulates debate around Scotland's future, the issues affecting the country and how we can ensure our future economic and cultural success.

This anthology demonstrates that Scotland's literary and cultural success is not just a thing of the past. While we celebrate Burns' legacy throughout 2009, it is also a year for looking ahead. In celebrating our past we must also have an eye to the future, supporting and investing in our assets and nurturing promising new talent.

Culture is the beating heart of this nation, it is very much part of the way we understand and project ourselves and Scotland's place in the world. Scottish literature and Scotland's publishing industry has a wealth of talent at its disposal to grow and develop in the 21st century.

This exciting roll-call of contributors serves to reinforce Scotland's international reputation for producing exceptional literature that both challenges and instigates debate.

First Minister of Scotland, Alex Salmond

INTRODUCTION

Stuart Kelly

In 2008, *Scotland on Sunday* started a series of features, events and articles on the idea of Scotland's Future. With the prospect of a referendum on full independence, and the first Nationalist administration in Holyrood, it was an exciting time to be thinking about the big questions. Representatives of every strand of political thinking contributed with a new sense of urgency and conviction, and the newspaper was proud to be the forum where the debates happened, and continue to happen. I was delighted when the deputy editor, Kenny Farquharson, asked me to assemble this anthology of new creative work by Scotland's leading literary figures as part of the Scotland's Future theme. Scotland's Future is not just a question of economics, constitutional settlements, demographics or voting patterns – important though all those factors are – it is also, crucially, a question about the imagination.

If a nation is, as author and political scientist Benedict Anderson proposed, an 'imagined community', then Scotland's workers of the imagination have been faced with a unique and inspiring set of challenges. From a medieval and early modern sovereign nation, through union with England via the Crown in 1603 and the Parliaments in 1707, to both ally and victim in Britain's imperial adventure, to a present-day devolved country within the United Kingdom, 'Scotland' is not a fixed and immutable entity, but a discontinuous succession of states, actively imagined in each and every generation.

In his book, *The Battle for Scotland*, Andrew Marr asked a simple and complicated question: what makes Scotland 'different' from England? One of his answers was its literature. Scottish literature has tended to be more involved in questions of national identity than its southern equivalent. Indeed, in the late-20th century it became commonplace to consider Scottish literature – especially the literature that was described by author and critic Douglas Gifford as 'the new Renaissance' – as politics continued by other means. Liam McIlvanney, son of William McIlvanney, wrote in *On Modern British Fiction* that: 'By the time the Parliament arrived [in 1999], a revival in fiction had long been underway . . . Without waiting for the politicians, Scottish novelists had written themselves out of despair.' The critic Cairns Craig went one step further: 'The 1980s proved to be one of the most productive and creative decades in Scotland this century – as though the energy that had failed to be harnessed by the politicians flowed into other channels. In literature, in thought, creative and scholarly work went hand-in-hand to redraw the map of Scotland's past and realign the perspectives of the future.' And author and critic Douglas Gifford makes the connection even more explicitly: 'It is tempting to see this change in confidence as somehow related to the 1979 Devolution referendum and the growing assertions of Scottish identity and its varieties that emerged almost in defiance of that quasi-democratic debacle. With this new confidence, Scottish fiction approached the new millennium as a standard-bearer for Scottish culture, arguably even supplying the most successful explorations of changing Scottish identities, in a rich variety of voices and genres. The new complexities . . . relate dynamically to the changes taking place in Scottish society at large, not only reacting to them, but influencing the framework of thought in which they took place.'

The idea that political despair after the 1979 Devolution referendum was alchemically transformed into cultural success is problematic. As Allan Massie perceptively wrote in 1998 in *The Spectator*: 'Talk of a cultural renaissance suggests there was an earlier death in the family. It's hard to see when that was supposed to be'. Any overview of Scottish writing before 1979 – including, for example, the authors Muriel Spark, Archie Hind, Naomi Mitchison and Jessie Kesson, as well as the poets Edwin Morgan, Norman MacCaig, Hugh MacDiarmid and Sorley MacLean – would suggest it was in rude health before Mrs Thatcher came to power. Likewise, if we accept the idea of the frustrated devolution picture, what happens after 1997, when Scotland did vote for a devolved parliament with tax-varying powers? At the time, there was a mild flurry of concern; akin to the idea that, with the change in government political satire would, somehow, become superfluous.

Some critics thought that devolution would allow a liberating normality to enter Scottish writing – writers would be able to explore something other than the nature of Scottish identity. In the words of the poet, critic and novelist, Christopher Whyte: 'In the absence of an elected political authority, the task of representing the nation has been repeatedly devolved to its writers . . . one can hope that the setting up of a Scottish parliament will at last allow Scottish literature to be literature first and foremost, rather than the expression of a nationalist movement'. Others, such as the *Scotsman*'s literary editor and director of the Edinburgh International Book Festival, Catherine Lockerbie, were more cautious: 'Now devolution has been achieved, people don't have to prove they are Scottish writers anymore . . . I think we've moved on from the days of the stereotypical writer. Young writers don't have to write those quasi-political novels. I think you'll find something more interesting and individual from them, rather than following the old path. The chip on the shoulder has been turned into a twiglet if you like and the Scottish cultural cringe has certainly diminished.'

In fact, Scottish writing in the last decade has neither atrophied without its mobilising grievance, nor has it been globalised into bland, homogenised mall-literature. It has not ceased to be Scottish, nor ceased to be relevant to Scotland. If the personal is political, then the local is also the universal. Many novels in the post-devolutionary period have been if anything more political, dealing with such diverse issues as Scotland's imperial past, the persistence of class antagonism, the ethically and sexually corrosive effects of the consumer society and the collapse of social cohesion in post-industrial communities.

In many ways, the situation for the Scottish writer has improved vastly. Unlike readers a generation older than me (I was born in 1972), I was taught Scottish literature and history at school and Scots was actively encouraged, albeit as a 'bit of fun' option rather than as an alternative to 'correct' English. Even in the rural Borders, bookshops offered a good selection of contemporary and classic Scottish writing – I well remember hoarding lunch money to buy books in the Canongate Classics series when they first appeared. In the past few years there have been published no fewer than five histories of Scottish literature, as well as several volumes of critical studies, guides to essential criticism and monographs on individual authors. In addition, genre novelists such as Ian Rankin, Alexander McCall Smith, Ricardo Pinto, Val McDermid, Denise Mina, Iain M. Banks, Ken MacLeod and Alan Campbell have enjoyed unprecedented successes.

The stereotype of the Scottish author has changed as well, as Lockerbie predicted. There are a number of high-profile and award-winning Scottish writers who are not male, white or heterosexual – or English language writers. At school, we studied Morgan with nary a word said about his sexuality, and the anthologies tended to stick to the 'Poets' Pub' canon of men. Modern anthologies are far more inclusive in approach – though at the same time the very fine writers of that almost-wholly passed generation (MacDiarmid, MacCaig, MacLean, Robert Garioch, Iain Crichton Smith, George Mackay Brown and so forth) are now available in complete, scholarly annotated and comprehensive editions: just as one would expect for contemporaries of T. S. Eliot, Dylan Thomas, Ezra Pound and Robert Lowell. A similar project in Gaelic has resulted in five exceptional anthologies, collecting work from the earliest period to the 20th century. When I first heard about the Scottish 'cultural cringe' – when I went to university in England – it already came with the vaguest patina of nostalgia and incomprehension over it.

Making connections between a country's constitutional state and the health of its literary activity is always a parlous endeavour. Events, as Harold Macmillan sagely pointed out to a 'dear boy' journalist, have the happy ability to keep on happening, regardless of which national narrative we might happen to believe. T. S. Eliot provocatively once entitled an essay *Was There a Scottish Literature?* Not only do we now seem comfortable acknowledging that there was, is and will be a

Scottish literature, we are also able to see how that literary tradition continues under all sorts of political conditions. In the 14th century, churchman and poet John Barbour was praising the heroism of Robert the Bruce under the new Stewart kings. In the 15th century, William Dunbar was using poetry as part of the dynastic diplomacy of an independent Scottish nation. In the 18th century, James Thomson was writing the words to *Rule Britannia* while Robert Burns was lamenting the infamous 'parcel of rogues'. In the 19th century, Sir Walter Scott made his own version of Scottishness a global phenomenon. In the 20th century, Scottish writers have been conservative and radical, nationalist and unionist, left-leaning and right-leaning, parochial and internationalist. In Carla Sassi's *Why Scottish Literature Matters*, she advances the argument that the critical interest increasingly taken in Scottish literature depends not on its being typical or representative, but on it being anomalous and resistant to neat classifications. Against this background, we decided that a new anthology would be an interesting experiment in taking the country's cultural temperature.

When we asked the writers represented in this book for new and unpublished work that was thematically linked to the idea of Scotland's Future, what we wanted was that anomalous, against the grain, imaginative and unclassifiable experience. The writers have transcended the brief. Nothing in this book is propagandist, and the most enjoyable aspect of commissioning, editing and reading it has been the sense that the authors have, instead of offering pat or clichéd answers, asked the deep and enabling questions.

Wondering about Scotland's future inevitably means reflecting on its past. Alan Spence's bravura performance, which opens this collection, skilfully and wittily reflects on the multifarious icons of Scottishness – a Scottishness both local and global, that mixes Belle and Sebastian with Jarvis Cocker, IKEA with the West Highland Way. It also asserts that, amid the various landscapes, artefacts, cultural representations and contemporary debates that make up 'Scotland', its enduring legacy will be one of thoughts, not things. Anne Frater's haunting elegy, *An Stoirm*, was written after the storms of January 2005 during which, in the Western Isles, five lives were lost. It would be a poorer anthology if there were not place for those who were robbed of the chance to participate in Scotland's future, and Frater's beautiful piece reminds us that there are values and events that transcend narrow debates about the political. William McIlvanney's *Burdalane* is also in the elegiac tone, depicting an old woman at the end of her life, contemplating both change and regret. It is, as with all McIlvanney's work, a portrait both humane and humanistic. In his afterword, McIlvanney discusses the genesis of the poem in his concerns for the Scots language, and the persisting 'DNA of Scottish experience' which that language allows. In *End-Sang*, W. N. Herbert's adroit contemporary use of Scots is also a meditation on the ongoing tradition of Scots literature, and the resilience of the language.

It was important that this book should represent all three of Scotland's traditional tongues: Scots, English and Gaelic. As well as Anne Frater's poem it is a delight that, by sheer serendipity, we have two very contrasting poems in Gaelic; Rody Gorman's *Aisling* and Aonghas Macneacail's *Do dh'Alba*. Macneacail's song can be sung to the tune *Hector the Hero*, and the Gaelic is accompanied by a translation into Scots; while Gorman's more experimental piece is followed by a translation into English – or rather into all the English words and associations captured by the single Gaelic word. The question of who we are is addressed directly in Roddy Lumsden's *Through A Raised Glass*. Lumsden ingeniously turns the question inside-out, imagining another poet describing the narrator's hometown. Is it travesty or uncomfortable truth? Is it an intrusion or a revelation?

Scotland's future, in its most literal sense, is explored in works by Robert Crawford, Andrew Crumey, James Robertson and Ron Butlin. Crawford – whose own poetic practice using translations of Scots has informed Gaelic writers – presents a fantasia on a future 'Robert Burns's World of Shoes', which craftily keeps its wittier and more skirling jokes almost literally down-to-earth. Andrew Crumey's future Scotland, thanks to global warming, has become a tourist paradise for etiolated dome-dwellers, albeit one with some very recognisable old Scottish fiends among the tropical growth. James Robertson's *MacTaggart's Shed* – well, it would give away far too much to even begin to summarise it, but suffice to say that his particular dystopia is not a million miles from many 20th-century actual nightmares. Ron Butlin's magic realist story takes the idea of globalisation quite literally, as a street in Edinburgh shakes itself onto other world locations. But with this surreally inflected setting comes troubling questions, about how Scotland is insulated from world events, how geology and climate determine behaviours and psychologies and how much we can change before we are unable to recognise ourselves.

If any one figure dominated 20th-century Scottish literature, it would have to be Christopher Murray Grieve, who adopted the *nom de guerre* Hugh MacDiarmid. One of his most famous poems, *On a Raised Beach* is perhaps hidden behind Kathleen Jamie's meditative, intense poem, *Raised Beach* – although she assures me that what was on her mind was a raised beach. Jamie's clarity of vision always encompasses the emotional as well as the actual, and her final line: '*Ah, you're a grown-up now / I've sung to you / quite long enough*', is full of hard-won growth and self-understanding, exactly in keeping with this anthology's overarching theme. MacDiarmid crops up again in a lyric from Robin Robertson, *Through the Tweed*, where the charm of the pun in the title is also a reflection of changing concerns and developments. The Tweed is an unofficial uniform of an older Scotland: it is also a traditional border between Scotland and its southern neighbour. Robertson's wry, precise poem marks a distance between the volcanic, creative-destructive energies of the MacDiarmid era and a more poised if no less powerful future.

Selecting the writers for this anthology was no easy task, and one that was made only marginally easier by my role as literary editor for *Scotland on Sunday* in that, over the course of a year of book festivals across Scotland, I was lucky enough to hear new work by a great many of the authors collected herein. One major consideration was that all the writers should have a substantial body of work behind them – the twenty-five writers here have more than 250 books published between them, and an ever-increasing number about them. This is not to disparage or undervalue the new and emerging writers in Scotland; writers such as Louise Welsh, John Aberdein, Andrew Drummond, Jen Hadfield, Luke Sutherland, Jenny Turner, Kevin MacNeil, Zoë Strachan, Ewan Morrison, Alan Bissett, Beatrice Colin and Elaine di Rollo. Rather, it was a pleasure to assert that Scotland's literary culture is both active and mature. We no longer need to 'discover' our own culture. It is evident in the extent and ability demonstrated here. As such, it was an honour to be able to include work by not only William McIlvanney, mentioned above, but the other writers who moved the literary centre of power from Edinburgh to Glasgow during the last century: Alasdair Gray, who is now concentrating on his visual work; Booker winner James Kelman (in 1994 with *How late it was, how late*); playwright and poet Liz Lochhead and university professor (and radical) Tom Leonard. Although Leonard is better known for his phonetic renderings of Glasgow speech, which ironically critique 'Standard English', the poem here is a clarion-like manifesto, where the narrator praises one who has 'won through to become themselves'; again, an aphorism we could all aspire towards. Liz Lochhead's new monologue is also about becoming oneself, in a more proactive and provocative way. It also addresses the question of gender, which, too often, was sidelined in Scottish thinking in favour of class. It's a great example of Lochhead's empathetic ventriloquism, and a challenge in its own right. James Kelman's story is recognisably set in Scotland – referring to contemporary politics, contemporary disillusion about politics and the harsh realities of economic stagnation – but as always with Kelman this setting is universalised. As the narrator says: 'Tomorrow is a brand new day. Except literally it was not. It was the exact same day as here and now' – an impasse similar to the dilemmas confronted by the protagonists in Samuel Beckett and Franz Kafka. Kelman's *talking about my wife* also shows aspects of his writing too often overlooked by critics: it is a piece rich in touching details about domestic kindness; bolstered by a linguistic verve and tenacious humour; and, as always, uncompromising.

Politics makes a more surreptitious appearance in Ali Smith's *Common* and Jackie Kay's *Mind Away*. Smith's writing is typified by its exuberant lack of the typical, and *Common* is no exception. In the debate about 'commonism', or 'human rights' in her story, Smith's sensitivity to language is paramount: these are not post-modern tricks or textual sleights of hand, but deeply aware moments, when the importance of the language we use – or are used by – becomes evident. Jackie Kay's *Mind Away* appears on the surface to be a story about the encroachments of age, but spins magically into a parable about identity and belonging. As with many of the writers here, Kay shows how learning to imagine is the beginning of connecting properly with a new and changing world. Likewise, Andrew O'Hagan's *Foreigners* explores, with his usual clarity and insight, how older immigrants can resent newer arrivals and how the progress to modern liberalism can involve repression as well as liberalism. O'Hagan has described the novel as a 'machine for moral meaning', and his short fiction reflects this as much as his award-winning novels do.

John Burnside's poetry, in recent years, has become increasingly concerned with unspoken, almost ungrasped points of illumination. In this major, long new poem, *The Fair Chase*, he presents an almost mythic hunt, and how an epiphany can change our feelings permanently and immutably. This is a Scotland of the personal and legendary past, shuddering into an altered future; shot through with epigrammatic apercus. When he writes 'in a country like this, the dead have more friends / than the living', it should prompt us to question some of the most enduring myths about Scotland, masculinity and bravery.

Don Paterson and Janice Galloway both address an aspect of Scotland's future which is subtle and straightforward: children. In *Jellyfish*, Janice Galloway's observant story about a mother's day out with her son just before he goes to primary school, a succession of possible roles present themselves, which only adds to her anxiety about what the future will hold for him. Don Paterson's acute and compassionate poem, *The Circle*, begins with every schoolboy's version of the future – outer space – before grounding itself in the quiet redemptions of the real. A. L. Kennedy's *Blackthorn Winter* also has a child as protagonist, though in the opening sentence the reader learns that an injury has already propelled him into adulthood. With her usual grace and insight, Kennedy elaborates on ideas of trauma and exception, epiphany and error. Haunted, perhaps, by Scottish literature's famous boy who never grew up, the story reaches a crescendo of steely realism and temporary forgiveness.

Finally, Alan Warner's genuinely smile-inducing *Blind Billy's Pride* showcases a more benevolent side to his skills. It's a story with twists, deft sketches, ribaldry and a generous moral. If there is one line in this book that has chimed at the back of my head throughout editing it, it would be Warner's 'potential vitality hidden in unlikely places'. This book is tribute to actual vitality in many places.

Is there anything not here? Well, the infamous 'Scottish Double', which critics have variously seen in Jekyll and Hyde, Burke and Hare, Highland and Lowland, Glasgow and Edinburgh, Realism and the Supernatural, seems to be taking a well-earned rest. Indeed, the rather unwieldy term, Caledonian antisyzygy, was coined to describe the supposed Scottish propensity to be two things at once. The term, when it was invented by G. Gregory Smith, was actually descriptive of the failure of Scottish literature – its lack of organic unity – and later adopted as a badge of pride by MacDiarmid and others. A syzygy, technically, is an alignment of planets; and Smith added the 'anti' to it to describe a more scattered, misaligned arrangement. Perhaps a new critical term should be made: *polysyzygy* – multiple alignments, plural connections, a web of interlinked ideas and words. Scotland's literature in the 21st century, on the basis of *Headshook*, might well be an example of the Caledonian polysyzygy.

The title of the anthology is another neologism from A. L. Kennedy's story. Choosing titles is never an easy business, especially in a work with so many diverse and different authors. It needs to encompass all the separate works but allow them room to breathe at the same time. Headshook implies agreement, denial, a surprise, a trauma, a startle, a shudder. It evokes new-found clarity as much as bemusement. It's a word that perfectly captures this collection.

What does *Headshook* reveal about Scotland's future? It shows us, first and foremost, that the future is not fixed or inevitable. Despite the various conditions of politics, psychology, economics and tradition, each piece involves a choice. It shows us that a future which ignores the past is untenable, and that if we do not choose our future, it will be chosen for us.

ALAN SPENCE

Alan Spence is Professor in Creative Writing at the University of Aberdeen and artistic director of the university's WORD literary festival. Born in Glasgow, his collection of short stories, *Its Colours They Are Fine* was published in 1977 and was followed by *Stone Garden* in 1995. His first novel, *The Magic Flute* (1990), won the *Glasgow Herald* People's Prize, and he has subsequently published *Way to Go* (1998) and *The Pure Land* (2006), a fictionalised re-creation of the life of Thomas Blake Glover.

An acclaimed playwright, Spence adapted and updated Sir David Lindsay's *Ane Pleasant Satyre of the Thrie Estaites*, published in 2002, for a production which toured across Scotland. His poetry collections include two volumes of haiku, *Seasons of the Heart* (2000) and *Clear Light* (2005), as well as *Glasgow Zen* (1981, revised 2002). The poet and his wife run the Sri Chinmoy meditation centre in Edinburgh.

A former winner of the Macallan/*Scotland on Sunday* Short

Story Competition, his work was described by the aforementioned newspaper as 'capturing that sense of vastness, a vision that stretches beyond the physical world'. His latest book, published in May 2009, is *Silver: An Aberdeen Anthology*.

TIME CAPSULE

Alan Spence

It's a beat-up old biscuit tin I picked up for 10p in a charity shop on Leith Walk, tartan-patterned with a daft Scottie dog on the lid, *A Souvenir Frae Bonnie Scotland* written in a stylised banner above the dog's head. The tin's a bit scraped here and there but the lid is a snug fit, should still be airtight. Fit for purpose. It'll do fine. It's a good size — maybe a foot square, four inches deep — and square is better than round, easier to place the things inside.

It was the kind of tin we'd get at Christmas or New Year when I was a child. Three or four of each biscuit stacked inside the paper floret of a little cupcake case. Bourbons. Ginger snaps. Wafers. Custard creams. When the biscuits had all been eaten, the crumbs and the packaging emptied out, the inside of the tin still smelling sweet and stale, of vanilla and sugary flour, it became a repository for domestic detritus, bits and bobs, myriad small objects that were too important or too finicky to throw away.

Old batteries. A bobbin of thread. Card of fuse wire. A two-pin plug. String. A hank of wool. Assorted buttons. A stub of pencil. A ballpen missing its top. Paperclips. A farthing. A foreign coin. A book of matches. A spool of undeveloped black-and-white film. A wooden clothes peg. A broken wax crayon. An inch of yellow chalk. A raffle ticket. A thimble. A nail file. A brooch. A button badge. A sheriff's tin star. The joker from a pack of cards. A tape measure, in inches. A roll of Sellotape. A single elastoplast. A payslip. A bankbook for a closed account. A thick rubber band. A chemist's prescription, unreadable. An opaque brown bottle of pills with no label. A key to nobody-knew-what. A postage stamp from Russia. A tract from the Glasgow City Mission with a biblical quote – *Matthew 6:19 Lay not up for yourselves treasures upon earth where moth and rust doth corrupt* . . .

I could have bought a custom-built container online – a sleek steel cylinder with a screw-in cap that would seal the contents tight, guaranteed to last for centuries. Or I could have followed instructions on another site, used an empty coffee can with a plastic lid. My charity shop biscuit tin seems a good compromise. I've cleaned it, lined it with aluminium foil. I've laid out a few things, now I'll see what I can fit. If the box had been bigger I'd have put in an old battered pair of running shoes, the coat I've had for twenty years. I'd put in the miles the shoes have covered and the winter cold the coat's kept out.

It feels almost formal, ceremonial, as I take each thing and place it. *No ideas but in things*. Pick up a notebook, an old-fashioned A5 jotter with notes to myself, a few haiku, a two-page short story, an unfinished sonnet, bits and scraps I've jotted down – found poems, snatches of overheard conversation recorded verbatim. Flick through the pages.

And is it after all no more than this?

the mist clears
and, briefly, the mountain
is there

We sang an old song and we made it new . . .

By the way, by the way, by the way.

The notebook goes in, and the pen I used to write in it – blue gel, fine-point. Add a couple of poetry books. *Sonnets from Scotland. Reports from the Present. The way we live.*

An artist's print based on a Latin maxim, an epitaph. *Sum quod eris, quod es olim fui. As ye are so once were we, and as we are so ye shall be.*

Another epigram/epitaph. *Non fui. Fui. Non sum. Non caro. I was not. I was. I am not. I care not.*

Here we go. Here we go. Here we go.

Pages from today's paper, just a few so I can fold it flat. Recession bites. Korea missile threat. Old Firm showdown. Talent show tear-jerker. I dreamed a dream. The cryptic crossword filled in. Sudoku (easy) finished. A diagram I made – family tree that only goes back two generations. Neither of my parents and none of my grandparents lived into old age. How it goes, how it went. They were, they are not. Photocopy of my birth certificate. A bank statement. A gas bill. A tax return. A train ticket from Edinburgh to Aberdeen. Boarding passes – Glasgow to New York, Edinburgh to Amsterdam to Tokyo. A wooden Buddha. A stone statue of Ganesh. A stick of Japanese incense. A splash of Issey Miyake. Receipts from Sainsbury's, IKEA, Au Naturale, TK Maxx. A

Caffè Nero loyalty card. A top-up card for my mobile phone. How we live. My diary. A memory stick. A photo of myself as a baby, with my parents as a young couple, all hope and possibility.

There were time capsules in Mesopotamia, Ancient Egypt. The *Epic of Gilgamesh* has instructions on where to find a copper box containing the epic itself, carved on stone tablets, buried in the city walls. Padmasambhava instructed his followers to bury Buddhist scriptures for the enlightenment of future generations.

It could all go on that memory stick – the books, the music, documents, photos, everything. An analogy for reincarnation, how it works. The experience of a whole lifetime stored, filed, saved, to be retrieved and downloaded into the new form we take. I imagine someone in some far future reading this, laughing at the crudity of the analogy, the reality of it much more subtle, at once simpler and more complex. (It may even be myself looking back, touched by my effort to make sense of things, of the lives I've lived).

Music, there has to be music, my soundtrack, from vinyl to download. A seven-inch single, a 45, The Who, *I can't explain*. Just as a reminder. Then a compilation on cassette. (It's partly unwound, spooled out. Wind it back in with a pencil). Joni and Debbie and Bowie. *Both Sides Now. Heart of Glass. Let's Dance.* The tape's just a C60, an hour of stuff. A bit of Dylan, Leonard Cohen, John McLaughlin, Zakir Hussain's *Making Music*. On to CD, another random selection. Penguin Cafe Orchestra's *Music For Found Harmonium*. R.E.M., *Everybody Hurts*. (Hold on). Cyndi Lauper's *True Colours*. Shining through. Nick Cave, *God is in the House*. Put in Pulp's *Different Class*, the actual CD, for the sake of it. Jarvis singing we'd all meet up in the year 2000. Sorted. Now it's all copied onto this tiny MP3 player, a lifetime of music, everything I own. From old blues, jazz, classical, Indian, Japanese shakuhachi, Balinese gamelan, up to stuff I've bought this year, bring it all back home with Belle and Sebastian and King Creosote, all of it shuffled together, playlisted.

All those TV programmes, the hundred best this, the greatest ever that, feeding the same need, endless nostalgia. Remember last week? The hundred best lists.

Sei Shōnagon's *Pillow Book*, from the 11th century, is a book of lists: *Things that quicken the heart*. The sudden sound of rain on the shutters. What it means to be here, alive, to be human. And what's writing, what's any art, but a time capsule? *Non sum. Fui.* I am not. I was. As ye are, so once were we.

Things that quicken the heart.

In no particular order.

Boats on the river. The late-night bus. Seagulls and starlings. The West End. Eastern Light. Glasgow zen. Glimpses and glimmers. *Hold hands among the atoms*. Atoms of delight. The light nights. Simmerdim. The *haar* off the North Sea. Smell of the subway. The scent of broom. An oystercatcher's cry. Heron at the water's edge. A hawk, moving/not moving, in the high air. Rain on city streets. Blue neon. A white rose. Christ of Saint John of the Cross. Kelvingrove. Bonnie lassie. The first time ever I saw your face. *The dancers inherit the party*. The music of what happens.

This swirl of particles coalescing as me. This wider configuration that knows itself as Scotland.

Grey granite. Red sandstone. Quartz. Gneiss. Schist. The Cuillins. The Cairngorms. An Teallach. Marischal College. The Wallace Monument. The Forth Bridge. The Old Man of Hoy. Devil's Staircase. Rannoch Moor. Glencoe. The Skye Bridge Song (Speed bonnie bus). Caledonia. (Old stories. Old songs.) Caledonian antisyzygy. A drunk man, a thistle. Solidarity. Divided self. Red Clydeside. Shipbuilding. Silver darlings. The People's

Palace. Poets' Pub. The Hampden Roar. The final score. Last
extra final times. The Declaration of Arbroath. A Forfar bridie.
The Falkirk Wheel. A Glasgow kiss. Inverness Caledonian Thistle.
T in the Park. Haggis pakora. A pie and a pint. A pudding supper.
Full Scottish Breakfast. (Deep fry the lot in North Sea oil.) A
hardened artery. A blackened lung. A pickled liver. A broken
heart. A happy hour. A bridge to nowhere. Now. Here. Northern
Lights. Holy Loch. The West Highland Way. Murrayfield.
Meadowbank. Banks and braes. Scottish banknotes. Scottish banks.
Flowers o the forest. A parcel of rogues. The Scottish Parliament.
An upturned boat. Piper Alpha. Flight 85 November. The price
of oil and gas. An absentee landlord. A cloned sheep. Clearance
sales. Offers over.

How it was with us. How it is.

Into the tartan tin with the lot of it, the hail clanjamfry, the hail
jingbang.

I've left the back room light on so it shines out, but there's
enough light from the big old full moon, clear and cold. The
ground's harder than I thought and the spade is old and heavy
and blunt, but I persevere, get the hole dug, a bit bigger than the
tin and two feet deep. In spite of the cold I've worked up a sweat
and it chills as it dries on the small of my back. Stop and stand a
moment quite still, look up at the night sky. The noise of the city's
far away, a car passing, bark of a dog, a drunken roar. Then it's
quiet again, in the cold moonlight, *the serious moonlight*, this tin
box in my hands, the sweat drying on my back. I kneel and place
the tin in the hole, let it slide in, rest. That sense of the formal
again, as I stand up and find I'm bowing my head, then filling in
the wee grave and it's like it's myself I'm burying, my own life
I'm letting go of.

I know I will die,
but still —
the full round moon

Hope and possibility. Among the atoms. Possibility and hope.
Here.

ROBERT CRAWFORD

Professor of Modern Scottish Literature at the University of St Andrews, Robert Crawford has won the Eric Gregory Award (1988), been shortlisted for the T. S. Eliot Prize (2008) as well as being chosen, in 1994, as one of the Poetry Society's New Generation Poets. His widely acclaimed work, *Scotland's Books: The Penguin History of Scottish Literature* (2007), was named Scottish Research Book of the Year in 2007 and described by *Scotland on Sunday* as a 'joyful, passionate and luminously intelligent guide to some of the finest writing Scotland has produced . . . He manages to make even the dull bits of Scottish literature interesting.'

In addition to his critical work, including *Devolving English Literature* (Second Edition, 2000) and a biography of Robert Burns, *The Bard* (2009), Crawford has written seven collections of poetry: *Sharawaggi: Poems in Scots* – which he wrote with W. N. Herbert in 1990 and *A Scottish Assembly* (1990), *Talkies* (1992), *Masculinity*

(1996), *Spirit Machines* (1999), *The Tip of My Tongue* (2003) and *Full Volume* (2008); his *Selected Poems* appeared in 2005.

Crawford coedited with Simon Armitage the *Penguin Book of Poetry from Britain and Ireland after 1945* and has edited anthologies of Scottish poetry, Scottish religious poetry and editions of work by Robert Fergusson, Robert Burns and writing from and about St Andrews.

BURNSWEAR

Robert Crawford

Welcome, Fifth Minister. Thank you for rushing
To open Robert Burns's World of Shoes.
Thirteenth of fourteen global Burnswear Centres,
We are the showcase for the Bard's old boots,
Pumps, cootikins, and miscellaneous footwear.
Fifth Minister, we're proud that we brought home
To Scotland for the Year of Homecoming
Those kick-ass metal toecaps that The Bard
Had shipped ahead to Ayr Mount in Jamaica
Where he once thought to do some work with slaves.
We have his well-licked boots. We boast a slipper
Slipped from the slim left foot of Highland Mary.
Professors may pooh-pooh their provenance,
But these stilettos of the Mauchline Belles
Rival the buffed-up, scuffed heels of Dumfries,
Clarinda's lace-ups, and yon nineteen socks

Burns never wore but kindly autographed;
Daddy Auld's lost galosh; Ann Park's wee latchets;
A front right cast by Tam o' Shanter's mare;
And best of all The Bard's own dancing shoes
In which he reeled and set and crossed and cleekit.
Fifth Minister, your own discovery
Of twenty thousand lost poems by Burns
Stashed in his left Nith wader sets us first
Among the cultural industries. Nintendo
Wii Sleekit Cowran Tim'rous Beastie kickers
Mark a strategic, world-class Scots renaissance
In Burnswear, and I hope that here today
Before going back to your constituency
You'll try a pair of Standard Habbie Brogues
Inlaid with toadying crowns and union jacks
(Said to be favoured by Sir Kenneth Calman),
Available in Old Fettesian
Blair Black or British Skint Kirkcaldy Brown.
See how they fit your feet, Fifth Minister.
They come gift-wrapped, your own parcel of brogues.

KATHLEEN JAMIE

Poet and non-fiction writer, Kathleen Jamie has won numerous awards for her work including, in 1995, the Somerset Maugham Award, the Geoffrey Faber Memorial Prize in both 1996 and 2000 plus the 2005 Scottish Arts Council Book of the Year Award.

Jamie is the author of seven collections of poetry including *Jizzen* (1999), *The Tree House* (2004) and *Mr and Mrs Scotland Are Dead: Selected Poems 1980–94* (2002), while her accomplished non-fiction writing covers subjects as diverse as travel in North Pakistan and Tibet, medical museums and, in *Findings* (2005), the relationship between humanity and the natural world: in summer 2008, her work was selected for *Granta*'s special issue entitled *The New Nature Writing*.

'Entertainingly nostalgic, compassionate and sometimes fierce,' Jamie's poetry, according to *Scotland on Sunday*, 'displays a deep lyricism married to intelligent and highly disciplined verse.'

RAISED BEACH

Kathleen Jamie

– of course, that's what –
a plain of stones, perfectly
smooth and still
showing the same slight
ridges and troughs
as thousands of years ago
when the sea left.
– It *is* a sea – even grey
stones one can
walk across: not a
solitary flower, nor a single
blade of grass –
I know this place
– all with one face
accepting of the sun
the other . . . Moon,

why have you turned to me
your dark side, why am I
examining these stones?
Our friendship lapsed.
— And sea, dear mother,
retreating with long stealth
though I lie awake —
Ah, you're a grown-up now
I've sung to you
quite long enough.

AONGHAS MACNEACAIL

The preeminent Gaelic poet of his generation, Aonghas Macneacail was born in 1942 on the Isle of Skye. From 1968-71 he attended the University of Glasgow and was a participant – as were Alasdair Gray, Tom Leonard, Liz Lochhead and James Kelman – in the creative writing group founded by the late Philip Hobsbaum: renowned as both professor and poet, Hobsbaum died in 2005.

Macneacail writes in both Gaelic and English and his published poetry includes: *Sireadh Bradain Sicir/Seeking Wise Salmon* (1983), *An Cathadh Mor/The Great Snowbattle* (1984), *An Seachnadh/The Avoiding* (1986), *Rock and Water* (1990), *Oideachadh Ceart/A Proper Schooling* (1996) – for which he won Stakis Scottish Writer of the Year – and, most recently, *Laoidh an Donais Oig/Hymn to a Young Demon* (2007). At the National Mod in 2004, he was awarded the Bardic Crown.

Poet and songwriter, journalist and broadcaster, he has also written extensively for television and film, and co-wrote the screen-play for the 2007 release, *Seachd: The Inaccessible Pinnacle* – the first feature-length film made in Scottish Gaelic.

DO DH'ALBA

Aonghas Macneacail

Do dh'Alba ar dùthaich thoir miadh,
do thìr nan strath gorm is nan sliabh
thug tacar do dh' iolaire 's fasgadh dhan fiadh,
oir smiorail an cridhe na cliabh.
B'i 'n dùthaich a chùm a leus beò,
tromh linntean dubh breugnach nan sgleò,
air thaisdeal tromh sgoran 's ar n'anaim gun treòir
chùm i birlinn ar dùil fo sheòl

B'i dùthaich nam filidh's nan laoch
a ghléidh urram is athadh an t-saoghail
b'i bhrosnaich gu deasbad gach feallsanaich 's naomh
gum bualadh gach cridhe gu saor
'san dream a sheas cruadal is cràdh
is a chìr dris nan reachd airson blàth
a' chum beò ar dòchais tromh choirean an spairn
a' gléidheadh ar dìlseachd is gràdh

Aonghas Macneacail

Do dh'Alba ar dùthaich thoir luaidh,
cur a beusan 's a buantas san duan,
mar a' sgaoil i a h-ealain's 's a h-innleachd thar chuan,
mar shuaicheantas spéiseil d' a tuath.
Deanaibh dealbh a h-urram an ceòl,
biodh gach teanga a' seirm do a glòr,
biodh bratach a taisgean air fhosgladh mar sheòl
is slàinte a muinntir 'sa chòrn

FOR SCOTLAND

For Scotland oor hame sing this sang,
tae the land o green straths and high crags
that nourished the eagle and harboured the stag,
her lowe bidin bricht, crousie land.
Her hert she kep swack in its crib
doun the years whan her smeddum was smoored
as we traivelled throu daurk howes, our sauls withoot virr
the scow o oor hopes she kep trig

This land o great heroes and bards
has hained the respect o the warld,
wha steered saunts an sages tae flyte an tae thraw,
tae lowse ilka hert fae its craw,
for the fowk wha tholed trauchle and stound
and wha kaimed thirling's birse for the flooer,
wha happed warm oor ettlins throu the cauld heuchs o stour,
giein beild tae oor lealty and luve

For Scotland oor hame sing this sang,
put her farrand and macht in the wards
and tell hou she gied the warld her ain skeels and airts
as a banner o pride in her clans.
Mak a twin tae her wirth in fu cord,
ilka mou gie fu sound tae her leids.
Let the flags o her traisure be heezed like great sails,
and a health tae her fowk in the horn

FOR SCOTLAND

Gie Scotland oor ain land her due,
tae the land o green straths and high bens
that gave meat to the eagle and sheltered the deer,
for her heart is fou brisk in its fauld.
She's the land that kept licht in her flame
through yon daurk sleekit years happed in haar
as we traivelled through daurk cleuchs, oor sauls without virr,
kept the ship o oor hopes under sail

She's the land o great heroes and bards
that held fast the esteem o the world;
she prompted collogue atween halie and sage
so that ilka heart might beat free
in the fowk wha kent hardship and pain
and kaimed biddin's thorn for a bloom.
She kept our hopes cantie through corries o stour
and hained still our lealtie and luve

Aonghas Macneacail

Gie Scotland oor ain land her due,
put her smeddum and saul in the sang,
how she skailed her fine arts and inventions abroad
as a badge o regard for her ain.
Declare her esteem in sweet airs,
let each tongue shape her worth in rich words
let her treasures' bricht banner unfurl like a sail,
and her people's health raise in the horn

JANICE GALLOWAY

A versatile author, former English teacher Janice Galloway's most recent publication is her memoir, *This Is Not About Me* (2008). She wrote the libretto for *Monster*, an opera composed by Sally Beamish, while another collaborative project saw her working with the sculptor Anne Bevan on *Rosengarten*, a show based on the mythology, obstetric implements and processes of birth, for which Galloway wrote the texts.

Her most recent work of fiction, *Clara* (2002), won the Saltire Society Scottish Book of the Year Award, and her previous novels include *The Trick is to Keep Breathing* (1989) – shortlisted for the Whitbread First Novel Award and winner of the MIND/Allen Lane Book of the Year – and *Foreign Parts* (1994); short story collections include *Blood* (1991) and *Where You Find It* (1996).

'Among bars of darkness are spears of light only Janice Galloway knows how to sharpen,' said *Scotland on Sunday*.

JELLYFISH

Janice Galloway

A child was hanging over the precipice of the kerb, the lip of his pushchair pressing against his mother's thigh. Water scattered from a passing lorry, sprinkling his jacket-front like glitter. The boy tilted his head, rocking the buggy, himself within it, over the tarmac abyss. He couldn't be more than two, Monica thought. Maybe less. The rims of the back wheels, his sole contact with *terra firma*, were worn; the chair that held him, thin canvas. A juggernaut rounded the corner, changing gear so the pavement quaked like an avalanche. Monica watched the mother blink, draw her face back from the fumes as the words WASH ME slithered past her, close enough to touch. The boy, however, stayed put, the radiator grille as near as dammit tipping his nose, heat haze rippling his face into strips. The rabbit in his hand shook from the tremor rattling down his arms, his thin, green bones. Then the lorry, its lumbering, unimaginable tonnage, was past. Monica coughed. The exhaust at kid's eye-level. Carbon monoxide. Soot. Jesus, she murmured. Holy Mother of God.

Ryan tugged her hand. Swearing, he said. He was looking up at her, little face poker straight. That's a swear. Jesus is only for saying in church.

Sorry, Monica said. She tried a smile, hoping he hadn't seen any of the buggy business, that child dangling like bait. I just thought I saw somebody I knew.

Who? he said.

Jesus. I thought I saw Jesus and I was just saying hello. So it's not swearing. It's being friendly.

He looked back at her, considering the possibility of protest. He'd taken to being critical, lately. Monica thought he enjoyed putting her in the wrong, at the least testing her. Any minute now, he'd call her a liar just to see what she'd do. Cheating, she popped a mint in his mouth, sidelining resistance. It worked. By the time she looked back, the teen-faced girl and child were on the other side of the road, on their way. Monica felt embarrassed suddenly, judgmental. This habit of facing the buggy outward so all a child could see was only oncoming traffic and an endless stream of strangers was *normal*, after all. Everybody did it. That Monica didn't only made her a crank. *Nothing-the-Easy-Way Monica*, the health visitor called her; *that boy's got you wrapped around his little finger*. And though Monica said nothing, it rankled. *Normal*, mere habit and usage, had a lot to answer for. In the distance, she saw the little boy's rabbit fall over the side of the buggy, an elderly man picking it up. He held it out with a smile. Ryan's hand tugged again, drawing her attention back to rights.

Green man, he said. Look.

She barely registered the fact before he strode onto the crossing without a second glance. That everyone would obey the rules, that nothing bad would happen if he did too, he took that for granted. His whole world rested on a terrifying level of trust that shocked and moved her in equal measure.

Wait for Mum, she called, knowing he was already out of earshot. Wait for me.

Wednesday, at the tail end of summer, meant plenty of space on the ferry. She'd been looking forward to it. Their last day of freedom, a final fling before something momentous: his first day of school. The uniform was bought and paid for already: a blazer, tie and V-neck jumper, all slightly too large and grungy green; a first pair of proper shoes; a three-pack of shirts complete with cardboard inside the collars and far too many pins. Apart from the tie, which made him suspicious, he liked everything. Dreary colours and full-limb coverings meant growing up. At least for boys. She imagined folding his orange and lime-green T-shirts, nestling them away in a drawer as souvenirs. Today, however, they could wear what they liked, take a celebratory ferry to Millport for fun. Uncle Peter had taken Monica there when she was small, probably for the same reason. She couldn't remember much about the place now, just an ancient sweetie shop, sugar dummy-tits strung up like dead balloons outside, benches on the beach. But nostalgia seemed the right mood, Millport the right place for runaways in cahoots. Monica pointed out the slow line of family saloons bumping up the metal ramp, the cloud of gulls hovering over the stern, then fished his sunglasses out of her pocket and settled them on his nose.

You look great, she said. Like an explorer.

He looked over the top of the blue-and-red rims. Spiderman, he said. They're Spiderman specs. I'm Spiderman on his holidays.

She pressed his nose with the tip of her finger, said *Beep*.

Stop that, he said, as she knew he would. He swatted her like a fly. Just behave.

Gulls followed the boat for the whole short trip, skimming between water and sky. Monica had remembered to bring bread, so they took turns, like feeding ducks in the park. She held hers out, allowing the bolder birds to pluck the pieces from her fingers. Ryan threw instead, crunching his eyes against the wind to see them catch in midair. His skin didn't crease, she thought. Whatever he did with his face, it unfolded again, smooth as butter. When the bread was gone, they played I Spy, a game that had bored Monica stiff but that Ryan enjoyed. At least, he *had* enjoyed it, though these days, he more tolerated it in preference to outright boredom. They managed two games straight, then things became more subversive. When his fourth shot, something beginning with W, was not wind, not waves, but wombat, she gave up. I Spy's days were clearly numbered. After a trip to the engine room, the café and the slot machine, they resurfaced on deck for a view of the near-vanished mainland. Largs's steeple clock, shrunk to an exclamation mark, made the town look like Trumpton. Monica almost said so, then caught herself. He was too big for that stuff now. Playing safe, she pointed to a man in a hat holding an important-looking rope.

Is that the captain? he said, hauling his belly onto the ship's rail, feet dangling.

Monica guessed it might be. Ryan waved, tentative, but the man didn't see. They watched the island lurching closer, the people onshore waiting to return. Ryan wriggled, his feet swinging. Did dad phone?' he asked suddenly.

No, Monica said. He'll probably send a card.

Then again, he probably wouldn't. They dropped the subject, watched the harbour, teetering closer. When they were near enough, the notional captain threw the rope. A man onshore caught the hawser, looped and hauled, and the boat thudded home. It was neat, practiced. The business of safe hands.

Come on, Ryan roared. He jumped down, flexed his fingers. Last one on the bus is a dumpling.

It'll be me then, Monica thought, mock-hurrying. It's always me.

The back of the bus was the only place he'd sit these days, but at least the windows were clean. Single houses thickened into a row of bungalows, some with palm trees. The terminus, ten minutes later, was only feet from the sea. On the other side of the road, a chip shop, a pub and a pink shop strung with buckets and spades outside lined the road back. Ryan chose the sea, scrambling down the nearest grass verge. Reaching the rocks, however, ground him to a stop. She looked, trying to see what it was that made him suddenly hesitant. The trails of algae, maybe, covered in treacherous slime; barnacles and shale that looked sharp, tenacious, awkward to tackle. Abruptly, he turned and asked for a drink.

But we're just here, Monica said.

Don't care, he insisted. I'm thirsty. There was a hint of fretfulness in his voice, a need to withdraw, perhaps, and build his courage. She herded him across the road without protest, hoping they'd find the toilets soon. Inside the shop, he chose a purple drink. She looked at his white T-shirt and shorts, pointed, but he promised to be careful. He promised twice.

Okay. She handed over the coins. But you're buying. On you go.

After a moment's indecision, he put the money on the counter top and pointed: not a confident performance, but it got him what he wanted. Monica noticed the rack of magazines ranged at his back, awash with zombies and monsters, a samurai chopping someone's face in two with an axe. On the rung above, a woman with her legs apart showcased a little banner with the words MORE INSIDE in scarlet.

Here, she said, drawing Ryan away so he wouldn't see. Put the straw in by yourself.

It was a good move. Putting the straw in was a fine art by now, one he took pride in. She stood back, giving him time. First, he scratched the plastic cover over the little hole with one nail, then carefully scrambled the straw out of its sheath on the back of the carton. It took both hands, but he didn't drop the box. He poked the straw in, knowing from experience to stand back, avoid the spit-back of juice that was likely to result. This time, it didn't. He smiled, lipped the straw into his mouth and sucked, triumphant. He stretched out the boxless arm at forty-five degrees, its hand balled into a fist. Superman. Monica could almost hear the movie theme tune: the only things between the music and the outside world were the straw and the volume control.

He supermanned himself as far as the kerb outside, then sat watching passing dogs till the drink was finished. Nowhere to put litter distressed him, so they walked the length of the road, searching. Two streets away, still within sight of the sea, they found a bin attached to a lamp post. It was already full and spilling banana skins, but it served. Aware he'd done everything right, Ryan smacked his hands and looked around, thrilled with life.

Well, he said. What'll we do now?

Monica ignored the single purple splash on his collar and checked her watch. There would be no time for the crazy golf if they didn't go now. Saying it once was enough. They ran all the way. These days, everything was running.

The course itself was still there, no different from the last time Monica had seen it as a girl. One look at the plain concrete assault courses told her ricochets would be likely, but they could always duck. Her stick – a *ladies' stick*, the hire man insisted – was far too short and Ryan cheated, but it didn't matter. What mattered was the daftness of the thing, hitting a golf ball around windmills and through tunnels; Ryan winning by a squeak. They took the ball and putters back but the attendant was no longer there, just a man, holding a child by the hand.

Stop fucking whining, he said. You've had plenty, you greedy wee cunt.

The child looked sideways, said nothing. Three, Monica thought. Small.

Think I'm made of fucking money?

Monica glanced at Ryan. He'd kicked a woman at the train station not long ago for dragging a pup on a leash till it started choking, just lost his temper and lashed out. Before then, he had always been quiet, wary of strangers. Now, he was changing. Of course he was. He had seen her ordering teenage boys to stop fighting, muscling in to insist; ordering drunken girls at late-night bus stops into taxis to get them home. But seeing it in *him*, the added component of violence, had been unsettling. She certainly didn't want him reacting now, not against a hardnut who thought it was okay to intimidate his own toddler. The man narrowed his eyes at Monica briefly, sniffing her out. Then he yanked the child aside to let her past.

Don't know they're born these days eh? he said. His face was pale. He raised the boy's wrist as he spoke, high enough to lift him momentarily off the ground.

No, Monica said. She looked at the boy, tried to smile. Looks like you.

It was true. Matching leather bomber jackets, jeans, frighteningly white tennis shoes; both hairstyles expensively cut, exactly the same. The man kept looking at her, impassive.

I'm sure he's a great boy, Monica said. Usually, I mean. I'm sure he's—.

Please yourself, the man said.

He dropped the boy's arm as though he'd lost interest in the whole thing, and started walking. The boy, after a second's hesitation, ran after.

Monica sighed, put the clubs back on the counter. There was no one to return them to, just an honesty box and a handwritten sign. LOST BALLS 50p. She found some loose change for the hell of it, let Ryan slot it in the box coin by coin till it was gone.

Well, she said, drawing a deep breath. That man was bad-tempered. Her heart was still thumping.

Pig, Ryan said. A big, fat pig.

Monica said nothing. Nothing at all.

Back at the bay, an ice-cream van had parked in the bus bay, Tom and Jerry looking oddly antique painted on its side. Monica bought two cones with raspberry sauce as an added treat. Ryan ate all of his, dropping nothing, but she wasn't in the mood. A Jack Russell ate most of hers instead, then followed them all the way down the prom before realising there was no more. Sticky, they scrambled down the verge not far from where they had started. Monica found a rock pool and doused her hands. Ryan held back.

There'll be beasts in there, he said. Crabs and things.

No there won't, she said. For goodness sake, it's just water. Like in the sink at home. He stared at her. Okay, she sighed. It's not really. Let's be logical instead. She looked him in the eye, became a teacher. If there's crabs in this pool, they'd be babies. Right?

He nodded, once.

And if they're babies, they'd run away the minute they saw your giant mitts coming in through the roof. Right?

His eyes narrowed.

It stands to reason, she said. They're more scared of you—.

I know, he said. Than you are of them.

Clearly, she'd used that line before. Monica gave her hands another dip, tried to look nonchalant. The water was freezing. After a moment, Ryan dipped a single finger into the pool, making a perfect ring.

It's cold, he said. But his resistance was already less. Slowly, without breaking the mood, Monica stood and slicked her palms down the seams of her jeans, a demonstration of how to make his hands if not dry at least a little less wet. From the corner of an eye, she saw her son take it on, paddling, then dredging his fingers awkwardly over his shorts, unsure this was sane. While he struggled with the gaps between his fingers, she looked out across the beach. The water was glittering, sharp, the sand a fine buff-gold. Strewn across it, as though it had been upended across the entire length of the shore, was litter. From here, she saw tampon cases, polystyrene pizza shapes with most though not all of the pizza missing, empty wrappers and cups. Four empty cans, one wearing its plastic hoop, sat near a clump of sea pinks, oozing.

What a mess. Ryan stood at her elbow. He was pointing at a discarded coffee container, two whelks moving slowly inside.

One man's mess, she said, fishing the cup out of the wash, is another man's treasure.

What does that mean? he said.

It means, she said, looking at him like a conspirator, we can beach comb. And this – she rattled the whelks back into the pool, showed him the cup was clean – is for treasure. Okay? Anything good goes in here and not my back pocket.

His face brightened. By the time she had rinsed the cup again, he was already hunting. First hauls were cigarette packets, the gold lettering attracting him, she presumed. One had two cigarettes inside, dry as toast in their foil lining. Next, a piece of wet cardboard with a picture of a gun on it, the plastic mould where the toy had been now empty.

At least it's the right shape, he said. That could be useful.

Sure, she said. The shape of a gun is always handy.

It's explorers, he said. Excitement was lifting him now, letting a younger, less self-conscious boy out for his last adventure. Like on a desert island. He jumped on top of a rock, declaiming, I'm the doctor explorer and you're – you're somebody else.

Monica smiled. Nurse, the assistant, the driver, the pupil to his teacher – she'd been all of those. Now she'd attained the lofty status of *somebody else*. Maybe he was feeling it too, the way she had over the whole of last week: the encroachment of compulsory schooling, its undeniable rules. The beginning of separateness. This time tomorrow, he'd still be four years old, but he'd be in uniform, preparing to take on the outside world. She watched him then, running on the shale, all fear of falling forgotten. He had no idea, she thought, shivering as a chill breeze caught her neck, how vulnerable he seemed. Of course not. He was an explorer, unstoppable. Already he had found something new, was waving for her to come. She scrambled towards him, looked. He pointed into a nest of discarded razor-shells and polythene bags at something pallid. She picked it up, turned it in her hands. It was bone. A tiny pelvis, almost; two empty empty sockets and a bowl the colour of clotted cream, dried weed clinging to its hollows.

It's a skull for horses, he whispered.

She looked at him, wondering where that had come from.

It is, he said. I've seen them before.

It's awful small for a horse, she whispered back.

He got down on his hunkers, looked her in the eye. That's because it's shrunk.

His face was professorial. Monica tried not to laugh. Mere *somebody else*, she was in no position to argue.

Well, doctor, she said. If you say so, that's what it is.

She dropped it with the rest into the cup. The rest of the beach gave them four silvery feathers, orange pebbles, a handful of jointed shells, a doll's head with no eyes, a cache of egg cases, a single crab claw and a single sock, baby-sized, that seemed to have been chewed. Last, he found some glass pebbles, glycerine-clear till lifted from the water, when they turned a cloudy green. Nearby were more in brown and white. Ryan stared and shook his head.

Are they *real* treasure? he said. Opals or something?

The word *maybe* was hovering on the tip of her tongue. She fought with it, then decided better. No. Uncle Peter had done the very same. It's bits of glass, she said. People bring bottles down here, then the bottles get smashed. And over a long, long time, with the sand and rocks and things, the pieces of glass get worn smooth. She remembered her uncle's face explaining, how little it had looked like her mother's. Then they end up like this. She held one out in her palm. See?

Ryan picked it up, drew one finger across its side. No blood, he said. Glass that doesn't cut. Their eyes met. That's sort of magic, he said. So it's okay. Magic's worth money.

Between magic and money, the stage he was at. A whole new boy was coming up to meet her, someone surprising. He laughed as he gathered them together, his baby teeth near-transparent in the clear light. Monica slipped the whole lot into her back pocket, aware she'd said she wouldn't do anything of the sort.

Caught me, she said. He grinned.

*　　*　　*

They turned at the natural conclusion of the sand. Out past the range of offshore hills, rain was misting in from the mainland. Ryan ran ahead, then stopped sharply, poking one slatted shoe out in front of him. Monica thought he was trying to avoid the grit getting into his sandals to begin with, the sand having turned again to shale. Closer, she saw little round patties, like eggs left to dry in the sun, slumped on the pitted shoreline. Ryan's eyes were round.

Jellyfish, she said. Ryan looked worried. They're animals, she said.

You can see through them, he said, horrified. Into their guts.

It was true. Pebbles were clearly visible beneath the sprawled, plasma-yellow bodies, tinted to match. Monica poked one with the tip of her sandal, dusting the gummy surface with sand.

It's still an animal, she said. They live in the water most of the time, floating. But if the tide turns too fast, they get stuck.

It's got no legs, he said.

No fins, she added. Just this.

He nodded, all trust, then scanned the beach. Feet away were more, bigger and uglier. One, the biggest, had a rock in the middle and was bust to bits, its body turning cloudy. This close it looked liked a blood clot under slow-frying albumen, an eye in need of surgery.

Is it sore? he said, slowly.

It's dying, Monica said. Maybe dead already. That's why it's going white.

Ryan kept looking, horrified. Why?

This was a hard one. Monica took a deep breath.

Well, she said, sometimes people aren't good. They attack things that can't fight back.

Why?

Maybe they don't think hard enough. She hoped he wouldn't get stuck on a *why?* groove. Answers here were not easy.

But it can't run away, he said. They should take it back in the water. They should behave.

Yes, they should. But they don't. Maybe they hurt it—, her voice faltered, —they hurt it *just because* it can't stop them. And because they can.

Ryan's face grew dark. Monica bit her lip. She was too soft, her mother said. She'd pass that on if she wasn't careful, make her own son into bully-fodder. Actually, her mother had used a cruder word, a word that drove Monica crazy, but the advice itself was not so easy to dismiss. She fought it now, aware something this slight made her weak. These soft, transparent animals, open as wounds, lying where the tide settled them to simply wait. Stranded, they had no defences. Nothing. She could have wept.

Maybe, she said. Maybe they don't feel pain the way people do.

Her voice petered out. She couldn't think of anything else to say. They stood together a little longer, looking down. Then Ryan made a move. With no telling what made the choice, he started running. That was new too. He charged at things these days, just ran. He ran all the time, refusing to hold her hand. She hoped she'd remember that tomorrow, not be selfish. *On the way to school, do not hold his hand. Do not cry and do not hold his hand.* Suddenly, the ice-cream dog appeared from nowhere and ran beside him, thrilled to bits. Monica sniffed. Ryan was sociable, not like her. He'd run till he was tired. Then he'd come back. There was no need to follow, no need to worry. He'd be back.

On the other side of the dunes, a couple of toddlers were digging. Not far away, someone that might be their big sister was struggling towards them with a filled pail, spilling water that made moon-holes on the sand. She watched for a moment, then realised there was more to it. The sand itself. There was something about the sand itself on this stretch of beach. Mere inches away, the line of her footprints showed it too, the sides of their sole-shaped hollows refilling, crumbling in on themselves as she watched. The sand was moving. Like restless crystalline demerara, these grains of solid rock were not done yet. The whole beach was tilling itself down as she stood here, moving on. Sands. She smiled at the thought. They really did shift. A tiny crab fought its way from under a boulder, waving his legs. She'd show Ryan when he came back. The day wasn't done.

She saw him then, her boy running back. Behind him, three older lads were kicking a plastic ball, squealing a commentary in unbroken voices.

Can I? Ryan was shouting, his voice all but blown away by the wind. He arrived breathless, big-eyed. Can I play with them? He pointed. They've a football. Kind of.

She looked across, undecided, trying to gauge something she couldn't put her finger on. They were boys. Just boys.

Oh all right then, she sighed. Why not? I'll shout you when the bus comes.

Ryan ran five steps, stopped and turned.

Did you keep my pebbles?

For a moment, Monica couldn't think what he meant.

The pebbles, he said. The magic glass?

She rattled her back pocket, nodded.

Okay, he said. He thumbed up, and went back to his running.

One day, Monica thought, watching him go, she'd get a camcorder. For now, she hoped her memory lasted. She saw his white shirt billow as his hand lifted, waving. He did not look back. His eyes were on the boys ahead, their welcome. They shouted him on.

TOM LEONARD

Tom Leonard is Professor of Creative Writing at the University of Glasgow. His collections of poems include *outside the narrative – Poems 1965–2009*, the groundbreaking anthology *Radical Renfrew* (1990) and *Intimate Voices* (1984, republished 2003).

In the year it was first published *Intimate Voices* was a joint winner of the Saltire Society Scottish Book of the Year Award; Peter Manson – poet and coeditor (from 1994–97) of the poetry journal *Object Permanence* – wrote that the works therein, 'speak so precisely and with such a fierce, analytical wit that they transcend their status as poems and become part of the shared apparatus we use to think with. I don't know any other contemporary poetry of which that is so true'.

In addition, other major publications by Leonard include *Reports from the Present* (1995), a collection of essays, political satires and poems from 1982–94 and a highly regarded biography of the poet and journalist James Thomson (who wrote under the pseudonym

Bysshe Vanolis), born at Port Glasgow in 1834 — *Places of the Mind: The Life and Works of James Thomson (B.V.)* was published in 1993.

A HUMANIST

Tom Leonard

The son of an immigrant, he had eschewed the culture of
his father as also that of the land into which he was
born.

The religion of his father was once the religion of the
indigenous natives, but they had rejected and over-
thrown it.

And the son was yet seen as of that tribe which corroded
the native culture and language.

An outsider, he felt at home with the art and culture of
other outsiders, for many years he found companionship
across space and time.

But from within he came to realise himself as instance of
the universal human. The universal human is inclusive
and absolute, there is no individual outside it.

This sense of the universal human is the home of all those
who have won through to become themselves.

And much trouble in the world is caused by those who
remain self-sequestered in their perceived province of
the exclusive.

ANDREW O'HAGAN

Born in Glasgow in 1968, Andrew O'Hagan read English at the University of Strathclyde. He is, to date, the author of three novels: the first, *Our Fathers* (1999), was shortlisted for the Booker (fiction), the Whitbread (first novel) and the John Llewellyn Rhys Prize; with his second novel, *Personality* (2003), he won the James Tait Black Memorial Prize for fiction. His third, *Be Near Me* (2006), was adapted for the stage by actor/director/producer Ian McDiarmid for the National Theatre of Scotland.

O'Hagan won a BAFTA for *Calling Bible John* – which he adapted for radio and television from his first book, *The Missing* (1995), based on his childhood. That he is an accomplished essayist is exemplified by two additional non-fiction works: *The End of British Farming* (2001), an extended essay published as a short book and *The Atlantic Ocean: Essays on Britain and America* (2008) – an analysis of the transatlantic alliance.

In 2009 O'Hagan wrote and presented a three-part series on the life of Robert Burns for BBC television; he is a contributing editor to the *London Review of Books* and *Granta* and, also, a goodwill ambassador for UNICEF.

Of *Be Near Me*, *Scotland on Sunday* wrote that the author's style is 'almost flawless: tone, nuance, the talent to surprise and the gift of capturing passing moments are all his'.

FOREIGNERS

Andrew O'Hagan

Aunt Jessie made a special effort to mispronounce our names, just to stress her hatred of my mother. She liked to sit for hours in the kitchen smoking those terrible Woodbines, chewing the air between puffs as if appraising the air's goodness to breathe. It was all part of some ceremony of impatience, at the end of which she would open her mouth to free a volume of smoke, followed by whatever unkind words had been brewing in her head all day. 'They have no business naming you all after precious stones, or exotic flowers, or birds from foreign places with giant beaks. I don't mind telling you: it's a piece of nonsense. They must think the rest of us were born in a sack of potatoes. Sean's a good enough name for a person, or Bridget, or else Fergus, like your Uncle Fergus.'

Even then, twenty years ago, Aunt Jessie loved to exaggerate. None of us is a Motmot, a Crocus, or a Yucca: my younger sister Topaz is Tops to everyone who knows her, and Lawrence is just Lawrence. Jessie has never spoken these names without disparagement: Topaz is Tonya to her and Lawrence is Larry, though she still thinks that's a bit on the flowery side. 'Now, I'm asking you,' she said. 'What in the name of the child Jesus is wrong with being a Fergus?'

'People only laugh at a Fergus.'

'Well, let them laugh until the air stops in their throats,' said Aunt Jessie. 'You will soon be ready for Saint Michael's and you'll sail through your mathematics and all the exams that prove you're nothing ordinary, laughing at people's nice names. I advise you to keep your brains immaculate. You'll soon be the very boss of your teachers, Amanda.'

'Amaryllis,' I said.

'Exotic bird. Coloured person. Whatever it is.'

My aunt said this and took my hand. 'Your lines on here are more Irish than Scottish,' she said. 'One of them goes on for miles. It is very bad. It shows the journey away from the Holy Cross.'

'That might be quite interesting,' I said.

The kitchen table was made from an old barn door and Aunt Jessie began knocking the wood. The television in the next room and the buses outside, the world indeed and its famous possibilities, were made silent for a while by the fury of her knocking. When the noise finally stopped, when Aunt Jessie's hand came to rest on the table, my lips were covered with a soft dusting of flour. A bowl of fresh eggs sat between us. They were Glaswegian eggs: more than usually small and white and not quite oval, they had shoogled in the bowl when the table was thumped. 'You'll keep a civil tongue in your head,' said my aunt. 'Heathen that you are. Coloured person. Whatever it is. I'm still strong enough to give you a good kick on the backside and watch your black eyes tumbling down the stairs.'

I was a child then, and could oppose Aunt Jessie only with an army of private imaginings. That day, I thought of the Glasgow eggs cracking open and spilling out of the bowl to advance over the old barn door. I thought of one egg after the other travelling to meet her fingertips, then moving upward to coat the skin of her arms and touch her face. Nothing would stop the flow of her catechism – not the eggs' insides, anyhow, which might choose to spread over Aunt Jessie's entire body in a manner quite unnoticed by Herself in favour of the Nazarene. Perhaps I would look south and see the egg running down her American Tan tights onto her carpet slippers. She'd continue to describe eternities to be spent in the bad fires of Hell, her sticky fingers drumming the table. I'd see her lashes slicked to the skin around her eyes, and she'd look surprised in the cold kitchen light, no doubt beginning to wonder why I chose that day to teach her the vengefulness of eggs. This all came back to me recently, when I went round to Aunt Jessie's house to give her a hand getting rid of my uncle's things.

'You never know when you're going to drop dead,' Aunt Jessie often says, and for years she has spoken about liver salts and miracle cures, as though being ill were a larger way of being alive, having knowledge about the dangers and making a little more room for yourself in a world of diminishing returns. Mother said Jessie must have thought she'd hit the jackpot when the doctors called her in to say my Uncle Fergus was terminal. 'What unbelievable luck!' said my mother. 'Just you watch her now. She'll never be back from Boots the Chemist. She'll be marching up and down the Main Street with a sad face. "Oh, my heart is broken," she'll say to anyone who'll listen.' My mother was never an easy person, mind you, and rather married to her own aches and pains, but she had a point about her sister's secret pleasure at the prospect of distress. Jessie had always been like that. She loved pain and its daily demands. She loved Boots.

As it turned out, my mother, Bernadette, began to fail on a warm day at the end of last summer. She went into the Royal Infirmary, and we knew it was bad when they gave her a room with a television. It was a hopeless operation, and she never woke again. At the drinks thing after the funeral, a bad-mannered old worthy from Ireland noticed that Jessie and Fergus were absent. 'Now,' he said, 'that's a queer thing, is it not? To stay away when they're putting your own flesh and blood into the ground?'

'It's not that queer,' my brother said. 'Aunt Jessie and my mother had no time for one another. That's that.'

My mother was younger than Jessie by eighteen months, though she preferred to call it three years. They grew up together at the bottom of Ireland, and Jessie was forever the favourite, 'the one with the great humour,' their father said. He never liked his second daughter: if she put a mouse into his slippers he would call her cruel, but if Jessie played the same trick he would laugh into the evening and stroke her hair. Jessie moved to Scotland when she was still a young woman, and I suppose my mother never stopped wanting to have what Jessie had. She followed her sister to Scotland, but then quickly married my dad before Jessie could help her. 'She wanted to be nearby,' Jessie said once. 'Which isn't the same as being close.' My mother made her disapproval of Jessie part of her sense of herself.

Scotland itself meant nothing to my mother; she never believed in the country as Jessie did. So, through the years, as Jessie appeared to grow smaller and more Scottish, my mother, the childbearing young pretender, became more and more foreign, somehow posher in her own estimation, even after my father vanished. Posher, perhaps, in place of being richer: my grandfather left everything he had to Jessie, the money from four Irish farms, and it paid on the nose for her life with Fergus. I suppose that's it: Jessie got the money; we got the names.

'You're a person and a half,' Aunt Jessie said to me when I turned up at the house. 'There used to be young women like you, ten a penny in County Cork,' she said. 'Nice white blouses. Curly hair. They didn't know the dangers, either.' Jessie was still formidable with her plaid skirts and smokes. I glanced around the room and noticed, through the arch, that her kitchen table was no longer a barn door but a metallic gurney from Ikea.

'Will we go into Glasgow?' I said. 'There's a new Chinese restaurant they were nice about in the *Evening Times*. I'll sort through Uncle Fergus's clothes when we get back.'

She looked at me as if I were setting out to test her. 'Right,' she said, and after forty minutes she came back down the stairs wearing a grey scarf and summer sandals.

'It's too cold for those shoes,' I said.

'My feet get itchy.'

'Well, sprinkle some talcum powder on them and we'll find some good cotton socks.'

'Is that what you lecture on at the university?' she asked.

'Common sense.'

'Ha ha,' she said. 'Talcum powder and feet. That's your specialist subject for those gullible Americans.'

'No, actually.' I said. 'It's Modern German Thought.'

She stabbed the air between us to underscore her victory and then wiped her mouth. 'I've got a good ointment for that,' she said. Jessie thought universities were meant for people who wanted to hide away from life, people who wanted to be special. For her it was part of my mother's one-upmanship. 'A girl like you can make the world stand on its head,' she said. 'But there you are.

You'd rather mark people's jotters and scratch all day on an old blackboard.'

'It's what I've always wanted to do,' I said.

'Nonsense. It's what Bernie wanted.'

'It's the best thing my mother did for us, Jessie,' I said.

'That's saying something,' she said.

She got under my skin with that talk. I'd been an undergraduate at Glasgow University and then I did my doctorate there.

'You've never budged from that Protestant department,' Jessie said. 'Now you're there stuck in Glasgow teaching every day while the world passes you by.'

'Life is elsewhere,' I said, just to annoy her.

'No. It's where you find it,' said Jessie. 'And nobody ever found anything with their head stuck in a book all day.'

I always drove faster when Jessie was in the car. It was good to show her the occasional thing she couldn't control. In the restaurant, the leaves of a spider plant tickled her neck and she complained of too much ice in her vodka. She wouldn't have wine and she hated fizzy water. 'Wine's not meant for the Scottish,' she said. 'It gives you acid. You have to go in and ask for Nexium for that if it gets bad. Or else Tagamet. That's the more common one.'

'Just one glass,' I said.

'Never you mind,' she said. 'It's the slippery slope for the Scots. They can't digest wine.'

'But you're Irish,' I said.

'That's right. And I'll never drink wine.'

She sat for a while making faces at a tropical fish tank. You can always tell when Aunt Jessie is preparing herself for something big. 'There's no need whatsoever for anybody to live like that,' she said. 'Underwater all the time. With blue stones and yellow stones. It's a piece of nonsense.'

'It's a fish,' I said.

'And who decides what colours they like?'

'It's just a nice thing to look at.'

'Not for the likes of me. It's just a way of making people feel depressed about their own lives.'

'Aunt Jessie, it's a fish tank!'

'Mark my words,' she said. 'It's cruel. Those fish were never meant to be here. They resent it. They don't like the damp weather and they absolutely hate the smell of food.'

While she searched in her bag for a mint, I noticed the gold rings had disappeared from her fingers. She said she had given them to Our Lady of Good Counsel. 'There's girls in the parish have babies and no husbands,' she said. 'Ten a penny, I'm telling you. Not a man between them.'

'Modern times,' I said.

'I'll give you modern,' said Aunt Jessie. 'They don't have the right shampoo. The babies' heads are jumping with lice.'

'Not all of them.'

'Yes, Amanda. All of them. All the babies in the parish whose mothers don't have men have lice. And there are no proper bottles to feed them with, either. Hardly a single bottle between all of them babies. And none of those cleaning machines— sterilisers.'

'That's bad news,' I said.

'I've never heard worse,' said Aunt Jessie. 'Because you can get things to kill germs, if only you keep your eyes open.'

'Sterilisers.'

'That's right. And the girls of the parish have none, so we're selling things up at the church to raise the money.'

'That's a nice task.'

'No thanks to the men, wherever they are. You've got to make an enemy of germs!'

Aunt Jessie formed a dirty look on her face and cast it toward a Chinese waiter.

'Tell that one to turn off the Calor Gas,' she said. 'The fire. It's too hot and it's making my ankles swell up.'

'Tell him yourself,' I said.

'No, you tell him. He won't do it for me. They like nasty young people like you. They're always trying to marry girls like you, girls with a nice clean passport, just so's they can get to stay here for good and sponge off the social security.'

'That's rubbish, Jessie. They're more Glaswegian than you. They were born here.'

'Don't you believe it,' she said. 'I wasn't born here, but I wasn't born yesterday, either. Those ones want your passport. They'll pretend to love you: next minute— they're off.'

'Rubbish.'

'Aye, well, Amanda. You just stick to your university books. Half the wee girls up at the school have kids to these ones.'

'Aunt Jessie!'

'I'm telling you. At least half. All the ones with no sterilisers. All those germs in the milk bottles. It all started off with these Asian ones and their fish and their liking for passports. You'd think there was enough babies in China.'

'Anyway. You gave your rings to the church.'

'That's right. Wedding band as well. Your Uncle Fergus had a good heart and he would've hated this business with the germy babies, just like I do. You've got to put a stop to ugliness.'

My boyfriend from America was the point of this talk. She would never mention his name, never mention Miami, yet all the time she was mocking the Chinese I knew she was really saying how much she hated Ben.

'People meet these men on holidays,' she said. 'They get drunk at those hotel discos and wake up with babies. That's what happens. Then the men come here, and after that they all run away.' Eventually I put my keys down on the table and told her to shush.

'Stop it, Jessie. God hates this kind of talk.'

'Don't bring Him into it.'

'Well, stop,' I said. 'You're only offending the Lord. Do you want to be doing that? Because that's what you're doing.'

'He's not bothered,' she said.

'Don't you believe it,' I said. 'God hears everything. And He loves everybody. That is what the philosophers would say.'

'Don't talk nonsense. They were all heathens.'

'Just the smart ones. But, anyway, the logic of the thing . . .'

She wouldn't let me finish. She just made the Sign of the Cross, then looked me in the eye with her wise look, the look that says, 'I'm about to tell you something you've needed to know for a long time.'

'Those people you admire all died of venereal disease,' she said.

It troubled her to think of Ben. There he was, this American, this man from somewhere she'd never visited. She examined the chopsticks, then placed them on either side of her mat, like a knife and fork, and, watching her tiny movements, I wondered what she thought. Was it just that the world was full of Bens, people not good enough for her niece? Or was it me that wasn't good enough for this mysterious Ben? My brother Lawrence told me that Jessie had rung him up a few nights earlier. 'He's actually a really nice guy,' Lawrence had told her. 'He's smart. Quite funny. He's over from America to study at the university. He knows everything about Stalingrad.'

'I expect he does,' Jessie had said.

'Be pleased for her,' said Lawrence.

'And has he a ring for her?'

'Get a grip,' he said. 'They're only going out together.'

'But she loves him, Larry,' said Jessie, snapping for more, I'll bet. 'She loves him to death. I can tell by the way she's doing her hair.'

Lawrence and I laughed for ages at that.

'Then what?' I asked.

'You know what she's like,' said Lawrence.

'Come on, then,' I said.

'Well,' said Lawrence. He paused. 'She asked if Ben was of the black persuasion.'

'She actually used those words?'

'Aye.'

'And what did you say?'

'I said he was African-American. I said that was how we talked nowadays. I said he was a smart African-American guy from Florida.'

'Oh, Lawrence.'

'I know,' he said. 'Isn't that a cracker? She just huffed and puffed. You know what she's like.'

I looked over the pot of soy sauce at Aunt Jessie. She was staring past me at the fish tank, and she wiped a corner of her mouth very precisely, like Mother.

Aunt Jessie liked to pretend she disliked all food except the stuff she prepared herself – tongue sandwiches, mashed potato – but it wasn't true. She loved restaurant food, and was known to chomp her way through the hors d'oeuvres with the kind of gusto that can come only from experience. Eating prawn toast and several spring rolls, she began to reminisce about Uncle Fergus, saying how different he was from other men. How decent he was. How clean. 'What happened to *his* passport?' I said. But Aunt Jessie didn't mind that sort of remark; she was familiar enough with her own bad character to find other people's quite convivial.

'It's under the carriage clock,' she said.

'Fergus Campbell,' I said. 'You must sometimes wish you'd married somebody with a livelier name in his passport.'

'Not me,' she said. 'You're all halfway up a gum tree with those horrible names. That's your daft mother, putting it on. I'm Jessie Campbell and I'll be Jessie Campbell to my dying day.'

The restaurant was quiet, fish swimming, waiters smiling, when a tiny crunch sounded inside Jessie's mouth. It was halfway between a crunch and a crack, perhaps more of a snap. Her eyes filled with tears as she began to pull out a long barbecued rib. My evil heart was pleased for a second, and then a broken tooth dropped onto the tablecloth, followed instantly by a pendulous exclamation mark of drool. I managed to get her back to the house in something like one piece; she was still crying and cursing foreigners under the porch light.

My aunt is not exactly a collector, but, over the years, she had made some attempt at collecting the Dolls of the World, and she said there was no doubt she owned the best ones. The collection started when she and Uncle Fergus got married, with a clog dancer from Holland which still stood in a paper box covered in tulips, forty-five years after the honeymoon. The dolls were kept in a large, custom-built display cabinet fixed to the wall alongside the stairs, and all the eyes seemed to follow you to the landing, each doll standing in silent testament to the trips Jessie and Fergus had made together. A Spanish flamenco dancer had sequins glued to her shoes and she brandished a black lace fan.

'What's this?' I said, stopping behind Aunt Jessie on the stairs to point through the glass cabinet.

'South African lady,' she said.

'That's a bit odd.'

'Nineteen seventy-six,' she said. 'Too hot. Rubbishy hotel, so far as I can remember. Not a very big pool. And that's the thing: your Uncle Fergus liked a good swim. He only went abroad for the swimming.'

For a second, the doll's periwinkle eyes stared right through me and somehow told me there was nothing more to say. Aunt Jessie climbed the last of the stairs, still complaining about her tooth. 'Now I've hardly anything to chew with,' she said. 'I used to have a whole mouth. Nothing was any problem. Steaks, Highland Toffee, you name it.'

Aunt Jessie first saw Scotland on a visit to Culzean Castle with the typing pool from Farl & Leckie, a shirt-making firm in Kinsale. She was quite high up in the company, head of sales, in fact, but she liked to take outings with the office girls because the girls had more life about them. Fergus didn't have a great job; he worked the gates at Culzean – I mean he took the tickets. Naturally, Aunt Jessie thought that was a very glamorous thing to do with your life, to work in a castle filled with pistols and swords, antique weapons once put to good use, she imagined, in holding back the English. She told me the letters Fergus Campbell sent to her after that trip to Scotland were the sweetest things ever written by an idiot, and on receiving the third one she began making plans to leave County Cork, saying there were always jobs in the world for girls with brains and a clean driver's license. 'Scotland is just like Ireland,' she said. 'Full of songs nobody knows the words to. And piled up with dirty bottles.'

I've always liked sounding out the details of Jessie's story. 'And you wanted for nothing once you were here,' I said, pulling down her bedroom blind to hide the rain and the memory of the Chinese.

'You wanted for nothing and lived in the first bungalow built in Kilmarnock.'

'You're just checking for Alzheimer's,' she said. 'It wasn't a bloody bungalow, it was a cottage. A proper cottage, with stairs. And it had been standing there since Robert Burns.'

There were times like this, when my attempt to show an interest in the family's past seemed challenging to Jessie, as if the interest could smack only of my mother's contentions. 'That's just our Bernadette talking,' she would say, as if to damn my curiosities and make them hostile. In our family, the past was more changeable than the weather, more ominous than dark clouds.

'Why did my mother come to Scotland?' I asked. I always had to think twice before mentioning my mother. It was as if I were invoking an ancient curse. I suppose I was afraid of what might follow— the usual litany of who did what to whom. But I was ashamed of myself for being so weak in the face of Jessie's weakness.

Aunt Jessie looked up at the ceiling as if scanning a map of the world. 'Because she was greedy for other people's lives,' she said.

'That's unfair, Aunt Jessie.'

'Well, Amanda— if we're using names! Don't ask questions if you already have a better answer. You're asking me, I'm telling you. Bernie should never have left Ireland. She had no good reason to leave. She only wanted to show me I was nothing much.'

'She's not here anymore, Jessie. Have you no softness about you?' When I said this, Jessie looked at the carpet and said nothing for a moment.

'She wasn't well,' she said, eventually. 'I know that. She had an operation and it's terrible to have an operation. They opened and closed her.'

'She died, Aunt Jessie.'

'I know that,' she said. 'It's a terrible business. But your mother would've died in Ireland just the same.'

'Would you stop, Jessie,' I said. 'She only wanted a better life.'

'Oh, yes,' said Jessie, quietly. 'We all wanted that.' The moment drifted off, and Jessie went carefully around the bed, adjusting the valance. She moaned to herself, poking a finger into her sore mouth, and when I went down to the bathroom she yelled, 'You won't find any Tampax in there!' I laughed at that, and laughed again when I saw the bathroom was just as I remembered: not a room containing a medical cabinet but a medical room, a health centre, a place where the world's most mysterious ailments might swiftly be remedied. There were pills for malaria and angina, though no one in the house had ever had either, creams for burns, ointments for bruises, blue and grey puffers for whooping cough and asthma. The window was blocked off with cartons of Tums antacid tablets, and there were bottles of disinfectant dirty enough to require scrubbing with their own contents. I found the oil of cloves on the corner of the tub; the bottle was undusty, the cap loose.

'Don't hurt me!' she said as I dabbed her gums. 'Some people just like to hurt other people. That's what they're like. Forever rubbing salt.'

'This is good stuff,' I said. 'You'll be ready for more lunch in ten minutes.'

Like an old woman in a Flemish painting, Jessie's face caught the light coming through the blind. Her eyes were as blue as those on the Dolls of the World, and she smiled in a manner quite obscure before turning to the mirrored door. 'It wouldn't matter to me if I never ate a meal again,' she said.

I've always been rubbish with people feeling sorry for themselves, so I said nothing at first, then I met her eyes in the mirror and couldn't cope with that, either.

'Did you put the sink in here?' I asked.

'Aye. That was me. I paid the man from Him'll Fix It to make a sink for your Uncle Fergus, in case he wanted to wash his hands in the middle of the night. Save him going down the steps.'

'That was nice,' I said.

'He was such a clean-living man,' said Aunt Jessie.

Next to the bed, a rosewood chest gave support to a stuffed camel, a family mascot with lashes as long as an Egyptian summer. Its eyes were amber buttons, seeing nothing, recording nothing, but the camel had started life in some far-flung bazaar, during our Polaroid days, when each of us loved the notion of travel, when together we planned the great lives we might live, for weeks at a time, in the world called Abroad, waving from trains, making calls from hotels, learning bits of languages, and going our own way. Aunt Jessie was never one for the Spanish Steps or the lobbies of old museums, but she loved those days of seawater and a bottle of tanning oil stuck in the sand. It was never a break from life but life itself. Aunt Jessie had done all that. But the image she now stared at every day was their one remaining landscape, *A Field Outside Dalry*, 1913, by George Houston, a local painter who had loved Corot. The painting hung opposite the bed, and it seemed in itself to describe the difference between beauty experienced and beauty admired. It was basically a painting of a Scottish puddle, but it meant the world to Aunt Jessie.

Fergus had begun buying paintings from Christie's when Jessie first came into her money, and, more recently, as the money ran out, he had sold them back. Jessie considered it a fair enough development. Fergus had been good at having money and was just as good at having none. 'We made sensible use of the pictures,' she said. 'Now it's somebody else's turn.'

'But that one's different?'

'Aye,' she said. 'That one's part of the furniture.'

Jessie seemed tired, but talking about the Houston gave me the urge to vex her.

'You don't regret the money?' I said.

'Not a bit,' she said. 'Your grandfather died too young, standing all day in fields, wet up to the knees. The money meant your Uncle Fergus could work at stuff that interested him. He liked history, that kind of thing. Brodick Castle. The Battle of Largs.'

'Tourist things,' I said.

'Don't be so German,' she said. 'People can be interested in things without sitting in a university all day.'

The silence that followed was filled with bad feeling, but it didn't last, the silence. It never lasted with Aunt Jessie. 'Amanda. Amaryllis. Coloured person. Would you itch my poor feet?' she said.

'Lie down.'

'I'm not going to sleep,' she said. 'Once you start that, once you start sleeping at three o'clock in the afternoon, that's you dead. I've seen it a hundred times. You start napping and you're dead in no time.'

I rubbed her feet, the tops of her socks. 'I'm quite the nurse today,' I said.

'*Die Frau Ärztin!*'

'I'm not German,' I said.

'No,' she said, 'but you love the Jerries. You're always reading those books. The brain-boxes. Well, I'll tell you something for nothing: they weren't brainy enough to hold us back at Normandy.'

'Who's *us*?' I said. 'You and the English?'

'Don't start,' she said. 'The likes of you probably wish the Jerries had won the war. Then you could speak German to one another all day and drive about in tanks.'

'Germany is not just about Nazis,' I said. 'There's more to Germany than that, thousands of years more.'

'I know,' she said. 'You don't have to tell me. I've seen *The Sound of Music*.'

Jessie kept some loose cigarettes in an empty Kleenex box. I saw her take one out and reach under the bed for an ashtray. 'Chuck me a light over,' she said. There was a glass vase on the dressing table, filled almost to the brim with books of matches. 'Give it,' she said. 'I know you hate people smoking, but it's my room and my lungs.'

Aunt Jessie took great pleasure in people's imperfections, and she was not frightened to admit it. 'Your mother had nice hair,' she said, lighting up. 'But she let herself go. She could have made something lovely of herself. Something attractive. She could've done that. Then maybe she wouldn't have lost your father so soon.'

I was stung by that, but I just asked her to lean back on the pillows and say nothing for a while.

'Too much air isn't good for a fresh wound,' I said from the walk-in cupboard, adopting her own style of medical wisdom. Through the door, I knew she would be nodding in careful assent.

'Aye,' she said. 'That's right. I've often heard it said.'

It was time to bag up my uncle's things. Jessie had been unable to face the task herself, and that is why she called me round. Somehow the day had made me dread it, too, the suits and jerseys, the old ties, but I wanted to finish before the evening. His suits were mostly dark. Seeing them in a row, I thought of him coming along the beach at Saltcoats years ago, an Ayrshire day hot enough for no socks but not for the wearing of swimming costumes. Uncle Fergus loved the beach and had begged my mother to let us have the day together. He wore a starched shirt and pressed suit trousers on the beach. 'That strip of land over there is the Isle of Arran,' he said to my sister, his arm outstretched and his finger pointing. I hardly remember the look of the island, but I remember the cufflinks at the end of Uncle Fergus's sleeves, the Brylcreem he used, and the way he washed the picnic things after we had finished eating and made everything so neat. He seemed like someone who had a grasp on life. 'You've got to make an enemy of germs,' Aunt Jessie had said, and that was Uncle Fergus. His dark hair gleamed in the sun.

The suits in his cupboard now had dust on them. Each one had the scent of expired warmth, which is death to me, and some had pins on the lapels: the Bowling Club, the British Legion, the Burns Club – places where Fergus had gone in his retirement to take advantage of the cheaper drink. He had never lived in the world of designer labels, Paris and Milan, but of small Glasgow tailors who specialised in charcoal-coloured fabrics, men's handkerchiefs, and hats made to order, shops run by the kind of harassed people that my uncle assumed were the mainstay of Scottish life. Yet the smell of my uncle's suits spoke that afternoon of a life given over to equal measures of piety and mockery: a touch of candle wax, a hint of sherry. I began again to feel sorry for Aunt Jessie. This was her life, and the cold suits were soon to be taken from the house.

'Don't get lost in there,' she said.

'Have you a plastic bag, Aunt Jessie?'

'There's a roll of bags,' she said. 'Make sure there's no coins in the pockets. Fergus was a helluva man for coins. If you find any, we'll give them to the chapel. They've always got a use for coins.'

Most of the suits were bagged by the time I found the letter. It was stored in an inside pocket, folded twice, with a racing tip –

Pride of Orkney, 4:30 at Ayr – scribbled on the other side. The coat hangers lightly touched one another on the rail, their jingle the only thing to be heard apart from the sound of Jessie's breathing. She was asleep.

I missed you at the car market. Come late tonight, Fergie. I get upset not seeing you. There's a few tins of beer in the fridge. MAY

It was a wild notelet from a perfumed box, and reading it made me think of school crushes, her name, May, scrawled inside a briar of kisses.

It had never occurred to me before then how much I hated those Mays, those women who mess about with men. They had no business doing that. I listened to the cars passing on the road outside and wondered how many of the cars were driven by liars. It seemed only decent to wake Jessie and show her the note, to let her finally put an end to this man and his clean living. I was almost decided: there was dust on my hands, the powder of dead moths. My aunt had every right to know that her husband Fergus had spent nights drinking beer with women called May.

The hall is the loneliest place in a house. I don't know why. Maybe it's the lack of truly personal things, the darkness of a mirror, the jumble of impersonal, old-fashioned shoes, the tangle of coats that are never much worn anymore, Uncle Fergus's favourite raincoat high and useless on a wooden peg. The rug on the floor has lost its colours, but perhaps it could recall former days, the pressure of suitcases left standing by themselves in the minutes before the taxi would arrive to take my relatives to the airport, the start of another great journey to the world out there. Everyone is always looking for something else. I stood on the landing and stared down at the empty hall, turning the letter in my hands once more, before slowly tearing it up and putting the pieces into my purse.

Going down the stairs, I passed the dolls' eyes, but the light was gone and I couldn't see their details anymore. It gets strange in Ayrshire when the nights draw in: dark at four o'clock, our trees frozen in the public parks. Jessie's cat came to visit me as I sat in the living room waiting for the evening, the oil of cloves open on the table, ready for my aunt when she woke with a feeling in her mouth. Mary the cat. She leapt onto my knees when she saw a cloud of breath. I'd never known her to be so cold before, but I stroked her beautiful back and leaned down to place a kiss between her ears. 'Ben's gone back,' I whispered. 'He's gone home for good. What do you say to that, Mary?'

RON BUTLIN

Born in Scotland's capital city in 1949, Ron Butlin – poet, novelist, librettist, journalist and playwright – is the Edinburgh Makar (the capital's poet laureate). He has written three novels – *The Sound of My Voice* (1987), *Night Visits* (1997) and *Belonging* (2006); three short-fiction collections – *The Tilting Room* (1983), *Vivaldi and the Number 3* (2004) and *No More Angels* (2007) and several collections of poetry, including *Ragtime in Unfamiliar Bars* (1985), *Histories of Desire* (1995) and *Without a Backward Glance: New and Selected Poems* (2005).

The Sound of My Voice was the winner of the Prix Millepages 2004 and the Prix Lucioles 2005, both for Best Foreign Novel. It has recently been adapted as a play for the Glasgow Citizens Theatre.

'As a fast page-turner,' wrote *Scotland on Sunday*, '*Belonging* is hard to beat . . . Lovers of fast-paced mysteries will find nothing lacking . . . It takes the finest features of the suspense novel, and combines them with the twenty-something metaphysics of Alan Warner. The result is both mesmerising and serious.'

UNEXPECTED EVENTS AT FOUR IN THE MORNING

RON BUTLIN

From time to time our street shakes itself early in the morning, stretches its length like a dog and then settles back down again for the rest of the day. Most of us sleep through this, of course – lying, eyes closed, in our curtained bedrooms, confident that our dreams will defend us.

It was McKenzie who warned me things had changed.

I was out for a pre-breakfast jog, taking advantage of the beach that occasionally shows up at the open end of our street. Enjoying the sea tang in the air, the waves breaking at my feet, I pounded along the stretch of soft sand between the traffic lights at West Preston Street and Salisbury Place. Given the heat haze, I felt sure we were going to be treated to something exceptional this time – no run-of-the-mill British seafront, but an Algarve *playa* or even the Mediterranean itself might soon shimmer into full view, while the other side of Newington Road and its line of shops faded to a distant blur on the far shore.

'Grand day for it,' McKenzie called over to me from the doorway of number two, where he was seated with tea and bacon rolls laid out on the top step beside him.

I waved back, not wanting to lose my one-two-three-four / one-two-three-four . . . rhythm. It always feels like an unexpected holiday when we have the sea so close to home, and brings out the best in everyone. Today, for instance, one of the peacekeepers had hung his machine gun on the nearby railings, taken off his boots, rolled up his trouser legs and was paddling around in the shallows.

'Goot run! Goot run!' he grinned and gave me the thumbs-up as I breezed past. His colleague ignored me. Despite the waves lapping his small traffic island, he remained at his post, standing stiffly at attention – uniform tightly buttoned, military trousers tucked into his size twelves and machine gun gripped in both hands. For him it was confrontation as usual, and a readiness to obey orders, whatever they might be. Rumour has it that our guards are part of a peacekeeping force set up by the City Council or else by the Scottish Executive, the EU, NATO or the UN – who knows anymore? – to keep the streets of Edinburgh safe for democracy. A final sprint took back me to the pavement just below McKenzie and his buffet breakfast.

'Tea?' He lifted the pot, giving it an inviting shake. 'I've always a spare mug for guests.'

'Love some, thanks.'

The two of us sat in a companionable silence side by side gazing out at the billowing white sails of the yachts tacking this way and that; further in the distance we could see a small fleet of fishing boats, a couple of container ships, cruise ships, a ponderous oil tanker lying impossibly low in the water. By now, some of the local kids had joined the guard frolicking in the shallows and were splashing each other as they ran in and out of the waves. Someone had set up an ice-cream stand, someone was selling hot dogs. It was a beautiful summer's day – *continental* summer, that is, not Scottish east coast – and the few clouds faintly smudged against the clear blue sky could have been erased at any moment without anyone noticing. I sipped my tea and breathed deeply. How I love it when the ocean comes to our street!

'Glad it's settled down again,' said McKenzie.

'Settled down?' The sea, I thought, looked calm enough.

'All this, of course.' With a wave of his mug he indicated the steps and pavement below and the nearby tenements.

'What do you mean?'

To be honest I was only half-listening. Mostly I was watching the holiday-spirit guard trying to encourage his colleague to lighten up. He'd inflated their emergency dinghy and, having run a T-shirt up an improvised mast and placed a cupped hand over one eye to imitate an eye-patch, was clearly hoping for a game of pirates. But his uptight colleague was having none of it. Not him, not Mr Official Action Man – his jaws looked more clenched, his back more rigid and his machine gun more menacing than ever. It would be hot out there in the full sun, never mind having to remain on high alert and accountable at all times to the UN, or whoever.

McKenzie turned towards me. 'I'm up early most mornings, remember. Our street— Well, you know how it kind of shakes itself—'.

'So I'd heard.'

'Like it's— like it's contented, you might say.'

He broke off to wave his fist at a gull which had swooped a little too close to his bacon roll, 'Get away, will you!' Then he continued, 'Just because the sun's risen every morning so far doesn't mean it always will. My theory is that when our street feels the touch of first light on its chimney stacks and roofs, it knows it can relax feeling sure that all's well with the world, for *this* morning at any rate. Recently though—'. He noticed my empty cup. 'A refill?'

'Please.'

He lifted up the pot and poured. 'Recently— Well, it's difficult to describe exactly, but just before dawn up on the roof—'.

'You're on the roof at dawn? You're joking!'

'Taking an interest in our street, that's all. Spot of milk?'

I held out my mug.

'Maybe I'm simply going off my head!' McKenzie laughed, but kept looking me directly in the eye. After all, who wouldn't prefer to believe the world itself had lost the plot, and not him?

'Not you! Never!' I made sure to meet his gaze for several reassuring seconds, then turned away for a sip of tea. 'You're as sane as the next man,' I added. Meaning myself, of course. But there wasn't even a smile from him. Instead, he invited me to join him up there the following morning. Better than trying to describe the indescribable, was how he put it.

By the time we'd finished our tea, the sea had started to recede taking the sailboats and freighters with it, and isolated patches of pavement were beginning to show through the thinning sand. As the opposite side of Newington Road came back into view I was able to recognise the familiar line of shops including Kenny's mini-market, the Wild Elephant Thai Restaurant, the florist's, the Metropole café and the Love Hate Tattoo Parlour, all present and correct. To make the most of the last few minutes of sea, the holiday-mood guard entertained the kids with playful bursts of machine-gun fire sprayed across the water to create a pleasing multi-fountain effect.

*   *   *

The alarm woke me at 4 a.m. The morning was dark, cold, and particularly Scottish. Maybe McKenzie really was off his head? What did that make me – getting up in the middle of the night to keep him company on the roof?

I shrugged to myself, gathered up my clothes and tiptoed out of the bedroom.

'Where are you off— ?' My wife fell back asleep before finishing her question. Lucky her. I got dressed through in the bathroom. A quick splash, and I was ready.

Rooftops are open country, wide open. There's no escape from the weather – the rain seems wetter, the sun harsher and the gusts of wind that tear across the exposed terrain, riffle the slates like a pack of cards. I climbed out through the skylight to find the morning was completely calm.

Once my eyes had become accustomed to the darkness, I was able to make out the shapes of chimney stacks, satellite dishes, TV aerials, and the edge of the roof fringed by the brightness coming from streetlights far below. Fixed between the two nearest chimney stacks was a tent-like construction of ropes, duct tape and plastic sheeting – probably the home of a refugee family, several of whom live up here in the hope of eventually being granted the right to come down to street level. Every so often one of the refugees takes a header off the roof out of sheer despair – and, really, who can blame him? The emergency services are always quick on the scene, of course. And so life goes on.

Beyond was a settlement belonging to one of the religious sects who've each colonised a separate dip or corner among the slanted parts of the roof – their various totem poles, crosses, crescent moons and so forth, standing out clearly against the skyline like so many elaborate posts on a drying green in need of washing lines. The sects hate each other and they all hate everyone else.

No one can tell them apart and, frankly, the roof's the best place for them.

'Give it a minute.' McKenzie kept his voice low. Last thing we wanted was to wake the fanatics and then be greeted as angels, heralds of Rapture or prophets – their various religious stormtroopers would take it out on us big time once the mistake was discovered. The refugees, of course, would think we were Immigration carrying out a dawn raid – the poor sods would get into a panic, gather their children, their pots, pans and mattresses and rush blindly around in the darkness – doubtless with tragic consequences.

'This way.' McKenzie took my arm. 'Careful – mind your step, loose slate here – TV cable.'

We scrambled down the nearest slope, stopping only when we reached a chimney stack that stood right at the roof edge. It had two pots, one small and one large, as if a giant – the spirit of the roof, perhaps? – was offering us cigarettes from his packet.

'Might as well be comfortable.' With a calmness clearly intended to impress, McKenzie sat down at the very brink of the four-storey drop, letting his legs dangle into empty space.

Comfortable? I remained on my feet, all but hugging one of the chimney pots. What the fuck was I doing up here at four in the morning? From over in Newington Road I heard the *pip-pip-pip* of the pedestrian crossing. No traffic in sight, no pedestrians either. Ghosts? Get a fucking grip. Non-existent traffic, invisible pedestrians – really, who cared? Hate-driven fanatics, refugees topping themselves, trigger-happy guards, a street with a mind of its own? – what the fuck was it all about? Suddenly I wanted nothing more out of life than to get myself back to my flat and into bed next to my wife, and be lying there fast asleep with the covers up to my chin – but that would mean first letting go the chimney stack . . .

'Any moment now,' whispered McKenzie.

Taking an even tighter grip of my chimney pot, I turned to face the east where Edinburgh disperses itself into the well-heeled suburbs and, beyond, to the reservations of the unwaged and unwanted. In the distance I could just make out a pale glow shimmering in the darkness, tracing out what surely had to be the very curve of the earth itself. It was a wonderful moment.

First light came rushing towards us. It raced nearer and nearer spilling across North Berwick, Cockenzie, Musselburgh . . . Within moments the bulk of Arthur's Seat stood out as a greater darkness set in silhouette against the coming of a new day.

McKenzie gripped my arm, his fingers digging in. 'Now . . . Now . . . Look!' He hissed in my ear, pointing down at the street.

I glanced over as far as I dared.

Abruptly, the streetlights flickered and went out. Flats, front gardens, pavements, parked cars, wheelie bins – all were plunged into total and utter darkness. It was as if a solid but invisible wall had been placed suddenly at the junction with Newington Road, stopping the dawn from coming any further.

Next, a wind sprung up out of nowhere and gusted the full length of our street. I could see nothing, but heard it ransacking the darkness, grabbing at bushes in the front gardens, tearing at the straggle of clematis covering the downpipe of number 8, rocking the wheelie bins. Soon it was hurtling itself around and around the tenement walls like an animal trapped in a pit. It was frantic, demented.

Up on the edge of the roof we were buffeted from every direction. All at once McKenzie's grip on my arm slackened, like he was letting go. 'I can't keep— I can't—', he yelled above the wind's roar and, at the same moment, I lost my hold on the chimney stack and tumbled headlong into the darkness.

Faster and faster I fell, clawing at the empty air and screaming out my lungs. There'd be certain death when I hit the ground. But then, just as I was about to crash land, probably onto the unfinished rockery of number 8, I felt myself being swept up by the rushing wind, lifted and borne forward by its strength and power – like so much debris carried before it.

At once, the familiar street became a dark place of pure and elemental energies whirling on every side. In the utter blackness I sensed the sandstone blocks vibrating with the weight of the massive tenements; I felt the tension in the windowpanes, their transparency perpetually arrested a split second before shattering.

Around and around I was hurled, faster and faster . . .

Then dead stop.

There was no wind anymore. No wind and no darkness – only an uneasy stillness like the calm in the eye of the storm, the darkness giving away to the faintest silvery-grey sheen . . .

The outlines of the skylight were first to emerge, then the wardrobe, our bed, the spread of my wife's red hair on the pillow, her face . . .

I was back in our bedroom. But how could—?

Reach forward and touch her, then you'll be really certain.

Our bedroom? My wife? These are *certainties*?

Don't think it, do *it.*

For several minutes I stood there unable to move while the light of early morning gradually seeped into our room, soaking into everything around me, giving shape and colour to our life together. Finally, I undressed as quietly as I could.

' —are you off to now?' Finishing the question she had begun earlier, my wife fell asleep once more. I climbed in beside her.

When I woke up, it was nine by the bedside clock. From the

regular tramp-tramp-tramp of footsteps directly overhead, I could tell that the rooftop guards were back on duty. I got up, intending to make breakfast for us both – only to discover we were out of milk. Shit.

I put on my jacket and went downstairs.

McKenzie was sitting on his top step in the sunshine. He nodded a greeting and for a moment it seemed he was about to say something. I waited to let him speak. Instead he looked away – and I felt the same uneasy stillness as when the wind had dropped to nothing, as if we were still becalmed in the centre of a storm raging unseen all around us.

No Mediterranean beach today, only the usual stalled line of double-decker buses and cars stretching back from the traffic lights, belching out their carbon emissions quota. Our two peacekeepers stood nearby, one of them on his mobile. No holiday spirit touched either of them this morning.

'Better get on with things,' McKenzie announced abruptly. He stood up, brushed the crumbs from his lap and placed his breakfast things on a small tray. 'See you.'

As he turned to go indoors he glanced towards the street like someone taking his leave for the last time. (But perhaps that's only with the benefit of hindsight.)

I was about to call after him when I heard a shout:

'Clear street. Everyone go inside.'

I turned to see what was happening. It was the guard who'd briefly set sail on yesterday's sea. He thrust me back a couple of steps with the muzzle of his machine gun.

'INSIDE!'

'But I can't,' I tried to explain. 'This isn't my house. I live along in number—'.

'NOW!'

An armoured personnel carrier pulled up behind me, more peace-keepers clambering out into the street. 'ID?'

'Not on me. I'd just come down to—'.

Sirens and flashing lights. Another APC. Men in assault gear, bullet-proof vests, visors, batons. A steel barricade was assembled at the junction with Newington Road. A helicopter hovered just above roof level. Our street was closed off.

'This one of them?'

'No ID. Says not live here.'

'I can explain, officer. We've run out of milk. I was going to the mini-market across the—'.

The guard was ordered to handcuff me.

'Cuff with railings?'

'Why not? If he's local, he'll feel at home.'

Like it or not, I was to be given a ringside seat of the action. It seemed they had McKenzie's name and his address. Forget the security system of bells and intercom, four heavy-duty peace-keepers took a battering ram to the street door.

BOOM! BOOM! The wood splintered and the lock gave way. They began stomping up the stairs.

It was then that I felt the air growing unexpectedly warmer. Warmer and with a faint but unmistakable salty tang. Hoping against hope, I strained to turn my head for a better view.

Yes! Newington Road was becoming sun-drenched once again, and the sky turning holiday-brochure blue! As the last of the stalled traffic faded to nothing, a stretch of golden sand shimmered into focus. It was dotted with beach umbrellas and there was an open-air bar made of palm leaves; near it, a game of volley ball was getting started. Shouts and laughter. And, of course, the sea.

Even though I was handcuffed to the railings pending some unknown threat, my heart lifted at the glorious sight.

BOOM! . . . BOOM! . . . BOOM! Three floors up, it was the turn of McKenzie's front door to get the battering ram treatment. BOOM! again. He'd have a mortise lock, of course. A gull trying to snatch at some leftover roll, scrambled into the air in alarm.

Next thing, *there* was the man himself – McKenzie, at his sitting-room window. Face distorted, arms outstretched and waving wildly, panic written all over him.

There's reggae music from the beach café, and a strong whiff of ganja. No downmarket British seafront today, not even a charter-flight *Costa*. This has to be Jamaica – the genuine Caribbean experience down to the limbo party I can see taking place outside our chemist's.

McKenzie's clambered out onto his windowsill, one of the peace-keepers trying to hold him back while another raises his machine gun and yells, 'Stop – or we fire. Stop – or we fire.'

McKenzie? The quiet-spoken man with his modest *al fresco* breakfast of tea and rolls, his extra cup for a guest, his genuine concern for the welfare of our street?

'NO! – NO!' I scream at them. 'STOP! STOP! It's a mistake. STOP!'

I manage to avert my eyes, only to catch sight of the more light-hearted guard offering his colleague a coconut with the straw already inserted for ease of drinking. He's in total holiday-mode once more – bare feet, baseball cap and Bermuda shorts. Paradise, or what?

McKenzie's scream was truly bloodcurdling. I looked back in time to catch the dénouement: the terrified man's fifty-foot plunge and his final impalement on the spiked railings. From only a few feet away, his eyes stared back at me in unblinking surprise.

McKenzie's body was taken away, the railing sponged down and my cuffs removed. I was let off with a caution about the need to carry my ID at all times. Surely I could now see that it made sense?

The steel barricade has now been dismantled, the armoured personnel carriers driven off – for our continued comfort and security, the two peacekeepers remain behind.

So here I am, a free man once more. Should I go upstairs to tell my wife about this morning's tragic events? Or have a quick paddle in the sea first, to calm me?

Wait . . . Was it my imagination, or didn't the street give a kind of tremble just now, as though shaking off the last traces of McKenzie's tragic end? That aside, everything else looks pretty much back to normal – the parked cars and wheelie bins, the tenements with their small front gardens and, for the time being at least, a sun-kissed Caribbean beach only a few steps away.

Our front door opens, my wife comes out to greet me.

'I've brought our swimming trunks,' she smiles. 'Let's make the most of the day.'

'Thanks,' I call back. For what else can we do? What else is there anymore? What other day than this, what other street but our own?

DON PATERSON

Born in Dundee in 1963, Don Paterson has won the Whitbread Poetry Award (twice), the Forward Poetry Prize and the T. S. Eliot Prize for his collections *Nil Nil* (1993), *God's Gift to Women* (1997) and *Landing Light* (2003). His new collection, *Rain*, will be published in 2009. He has also translated the work of Antonio Machado in *The Eyes* (1999) and translated and reworked 'versions' of Rainer Maria Rilke's *Die Sonette an Orpheus* in *Orpheus* (2006).

As well as poetry, Paterson has written two volumes of mordant aphorisms, *The Book of Shadows* (2004) and *The Blind Eye: A Book of Late Advice* (2007), and an essay on the work of the painter Alison Watt (2008).

Paterson, who is also an accomplished jazz guitarist, was awarded an OBE in 2008. Of his work, *Scotland on Sunday* said he writes about 'love and reading and sex, politics, music and God, and all those other niggly riddles that beset our lives — male and female alike. He pulls it off with a blend of erudition and simplicity.'

THE CIRCLE

for Jamie

Don Paterson

My boy is painting outer space
and steadies his brush-tip to trace
the comets, planets, moon and sun
and all the circuitry they run

in one great heavenly design.
But when he tries to close the line
he draws around his upturned cup,
his hand shakes and he screws it up.

The shake's as old as he is, all
(thank god) his body can recall
of that hour when, one inch from home,
we couldn't get the air to him;

and though today he's all the earth
and sky for breathing-space and breath
the whole damn troposphere can't cure
the flutter in his signature.

But Jamie, nothing's what we meant.
The dream is taxed. We all resent
the quarter bled off by the dark
between the bowstring and the mark

and trust to Krishna or to fate
to keep our arrows halfway straight.
But the target also draws our aim –
our will and nature's are the same;

we are its living word, and not
a book it wrote and then forgot,
its fourteen-billion-year-old song's
inscribed in both our right and wrong –

so even when you rage and moan
and bring your fist down like a stone
on your spoiled work and useless kit,
you cannot help but broadcast it:

look at the little avatar
of your muddy water-jar
filling with the perfect ring
singing under everything.

W. N. HERBERT

Born in Dundee in 1961, W. N. Herbert went up to Brasenose College, Oxford and now teaches creative writing at the University of Newcastle. His tenth collection of poetry, *Bad Shaman Blues* (2006) was, said *Scotland on Sunday*, 'deft and daft, part Dante and part *Dandy* – the closest I've seen to a classic since Goodsir Smith and MacDiarmid.'

Other collected works by the poet include *Cabaret McGonagall* (1996), *The Laurelude* (1998) and *The Big Bumper Book of Troy* (2002), while, among his critical writings, are a study of Hugh MacDiarmid's longer poems, *To Circumjack MacDiarmid* (1992) and an anthology of poetic manifestos, *Strong Words: Modern Poets on Modern Poetry* (2000).

Herbert pens his work in both English and Scots but he has written that, 'Scots is a language capable of doing more than English, capable of doing something different from English that criticises and, ultimately, extends English. That is the spirit in which I write Scots poetry.'

W. N. Herbert

His work has been described in *Scotland on Sunday* thus, 'In some ways Herbert resembles a surfer. Other poets might go diving for miniscule pearls, or describe their beautiful yacht, or stay on the beach yearning for the ocean; but he's the one out there, sometimes falling off, sometimes larking around, sometimes coming in to shore beautifully, but always conveying the sense that it's more exciting at the edge.'

END-SANG

W. N. Herbert

Noo aa thi seas rin dreh, ma luve,
lyk seevin gantin whales,
and ilka feech-choakt thrapple's coughed
uts final scrip o sail:

Cresseid quos ane, and *crammasy*,
and *speshlʒ* croaks a third –
sae ilka sang Eh sung tae thee's
a threid o lang-droont wurds.

And noo thi rocks hae meltit back
lyk lips and lea nae bane,
thi sun's a rosie in thi dark
sae nane shall see tae sain:

Auld Reekie's graned, and *stretterhawl*,
anither crehs *Kilmeny* —
sae ilka sonnet's net's been trawled
fur oor leid's blude-reid penny.

And as thi ainguls fae thi lift
lyk ashy keys descend,
ae last commandment is oor gift:
lyk *pillie wantons*, end.

RODY GORMAN

Poet and translator Rody Gorman was born in Dublin, Ireland in 1960 and since the mid-80s has lived on the Isle of Skye and has been a writing fellow at the island's Gaelic-speaking further education college, Sabhal Mòr Ostaig; he also edits the annual Irish and Scottish Gaelic poetry anthology *An Guth*.

Gorman writes in English and in Gaelic – both Irish and Scottish. His published poetry collections include: *Fax and Other Poems* (1996); *Cùis-Ghaoil* and *Bealach Garbh* (both in 1999); *Air a' Charbad fo Thalamh/On the Underground* (2000); *Naomhóga na Laoi* (2003); *Tóithín ag Tláithínteacht* and *An Duilleog agus an Crotal* (both in 2004); *Flora from Lusitania* (2005) and *Zonda? Khamsin? Sharaav? Camanchaca?* (2006).

His translations into Gaelic include works by poets as diverse as W. B. Yeats, Patrick Kavanagh, Philip Larkin and the scientist/poet Miroslav Holub – and Gorman has also collaborated on Gaelic translations of songs by Bob Dylan.

Rody Gorman

Praising *Fax and Other Poems*, *Scotland on Sunday* wrote, 'the poems also give the impression that Gorman does not have to agonise over his choices of words; that it all comes easily.'

AISLING

Rody Gorman

Alba bhuam air fàire,
'S ann a bhios mi gur faicinn
Gu cruinn fhathast bhon tobhta
Far an robh 'n teaghlach agam san làthair
Anns an aimsir a dh'fhalbh –
Fàs is beathaichean gun àireamh,
Am bearradh fada fo bhlàth
'S mo chridhe bochd fhèin ri leaghadh,
An saoghal coimheach
Duaichnidh 's bàn le chèile,
Balbh is bodhar
A leithid a cheumannan fodha
Na Thìr-fo-Thuinn
An aomadh a' Chuain Sgìth.

Rody Gorman

DREAMNIGHTMAREAISLING
WOMANVISIONPOEM

O Scotlandalpinewhite farawaywanting from me on the
horizonridge in the offing I canwill see youall
globepreciselyassembled againstill from the turfwallthwart-
knollruin where my racefamilyhouse was
victorylocationpresent in the epochseasonweathertime that
has walkevacuated – wastegrowth and
unthinkableinnumerable livingbrutecreatures, the long
cuttingridgeprecipice long in
warmgreenfieldconsequencebloom and my poordearsadsick
heart nearmelting, in a safealienfierce
livingageuniverseworld terribly uglydeformeddismalblack
and fallowgroundvacantwhite bothtogether,
dumbatpeacequiet and heavydeafstagnentsilent so many
limpsteppathdegrees below, a
Tireeatlantisunderthewaveland in the fallingseasurface of
the tiredoceanMinchbay.

ALASDAIR GRAY

Artist, novelist, writer of short stories, poet, dramatist, polemicist and national treasure, Alasdair Gray was born in Riddrie, East Glasgow in 1934. His debut novel, *Lanark: a Life in Four Books* (1981) is widely considered a contemporary classic, and he won the *Guardian* Fiction Prize for *Poor Things* (1992).

Among the great polymath's prolific writings are the short story collection *Unlikely Stories, Mostly* (1983), the novel *1982, Janine* (1984) and *The Book of Prefaces* (2000) – an anthology, *A Short History of Literary Thought in Words by Great Writers of Four Nations From the 7th Century to the 20th Century*, of which Gray is author and editor. The author's published writing over the past few years includes the novel *Old Men in Love* (2007) and his 'imitation' – a comedy play in verse – of Goethe's Faust myth entitled *Fleck* (2008). Gray is currently working on an autobiographical catalogue – or, more accurately, pictobiography – *A Life in Pictures*.

His visual art includes the vast and most ambitious mural

adornment of Glasgow's Òran Mór arts centre – and there are many more on the city's walls, including one, *Arcadia*, in the Ubiquitous Chip restaurant. In addition to illustration and painting portraits – including those of many leading Scottish cultural figures – in his painting Gray has tackled subject matter from sex and theology to booze and mythology.

TAM O'SHANTER

Alasdair Gray

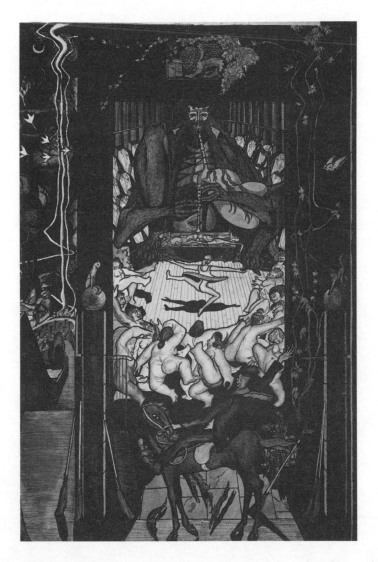

FAUST

ALI SMITH

Born in Inverness in 1962, Ali Smith won the Saltire Society Scottish Best First Book of the Year Award for her short story collection, *Free Love and Other Stories* (1995); her three subsequent collections to date are *Other Stories and Other Stories* (1999), *The Whole Story and Other Stories* (2003) and *The First Person and Other Stories* (2008). Of Smith's novels, two were shortlisted for the Man Booker Prize – *Hotel World* (2001) and *The Accidental* (2005). Her other novels are *Like* (1997) and *Girl Meets Boy* (2007), Smith's contemporary reintpretation of the myth of Iphis.

A play, *The Seer*, was published in 2006, and the author contributes articles and reviews to national newspapers including the *Guardian* and the *Scotsman*.

Smith, proclaimed *Scotland on Sunday*, 'writes in the modernist tradition of Joyce or Beckett, a literature that looks backward to Dickens and the Victorians as well as forward to the unwritten future.'

COMMON

Ali Smith

Hugh Whittaker loved his wife. He knew for a fact. It was true, Hugh knew, because at the exact moment his Achilles tendon had snapped he had simply forgiven her. You see? *Before* he knew what had happened! *I forgive her.*

And it was spring, it was Sunday just before lunch, it was a bloody marvellous day out there. A bird outside was repeating itself. Hugh Hugh Hugh, it called.

It didn't matter that the Achilles tendon snapping had been nothing to do with Katharine. It didn't matter that, in reality, as he'd discovered at A&E, and as the surgeon had told him repeatedly, it was a plantar problem, it was probably his not stretching properly for years that had made it happen. Hugh knew what mattered now, and the real fact of the matter was this. In the split second when all he'd known was the kicked-by-the-invisible-horse-in-the-back-of-the-leg of it, the precise moment that his brain reasoned that Katharine (who had been a hundred yards away in reality, back in the car park, doing something at the boot of the car) *of course* was to blame, *had* to be to blame, *must* have caught him in the back of his calf with the toe of one of her prohibitively expensive shoes or the knife-sharp point of the shoe's stiletto – he found himself thinking it: *I forgive her.*

Even now, more than a month and a half after, he was still astonished, and interestingly the astonishment felt very like admonishment. That two such unlikely feelings went together, sounded alike! Hugh Hugh Hugh, the bird said, or maybe hew hew hew, let's not get too, what's the word, the one that means you think the whole world revolves around you? Let's not do whatever that word was. It was a lovely admonishment, a lovely astonishment. It made Hugh giddy as an adolescent. It meant love. Lovely.

And when in his life had Hugh ever felt so at home with a word like *lovely*? Hugh laughed. Haw! He rattled the whole newspaper with his guffaw. He wondered if Katharine, in the kitchen, heard him. He did the laugh again, a bit louder, rattled the paper again.

And God, the loveliness of what it meant, too, after all these years, to find out that he was a fragile and precious construction after all. To be reminded that he was not unliked and the image that came to his mind, as he sat there in the sitting room behind the Sunday paper, with his plastered leg up on the table and his good leg there beside it, was one of a venerable violin, the beautiful neat brown curves of it, and not any old common-or-garden fiddle but one of the really important rare ones handled only by experts and, what are they called, artists, for centuries, yes, a bona fide piece of workmanship, something to be understood, tended, treated with immense care, whose strings might, at any moment, give.

To hold himself dear. He had forgotten how, until now. *I forgive me, actually, too, not just—*

Doorbell.

Hugh looked at his watch. Twelve fifteen. There was no one invited for lunch, was there? Had Katharine told him and he'd forgotten? No, because if anyone was coming she'd have reminded him to change into better clothes. (She was in the kitchen. She was making some kind of soup she'd seen in the *Guardian* magazine yesterday. She'd been out all morning getting the ingredients. She'd come home in a foul mood because Waitrose had no cumin. She'd walked past the sitting room and the mood around her head had been visible. He loved her. It was true.)

Doorbell, again.

He hoisted himself to his feet. He bent for the crutches, tucked the first one into his armpit.

I'll go, he called through.

No answer.

He swung himself into the hall. The person behind the glass of the front door looked Lewis-sized from here. He stopped at the foot of the stairs.

Lewis! he shouted up. Door!

No answer.

He reached to undo the top lock on the outer door.

A girl of about Lewis's age stood in the sunlight. She was wearing a flying helmet, the old-fashioned kind, leather and fleece with long earflaps. She walked past him into the house and stood in the hall. She seemed to be appraising the hall.

Hugh stood between the two opened doors.

Ah, he said. Em, eh—.

Lewis has invited me to lunch, the girl said.

Lewis had come downstairs now, on socked feet, silently, like some kind of annoying little cat.

Hi, he said to the girl.

Lewis, I'm assuming you've mentioned a guest to your mother, Hugh said.

But cool and oblivious as clouds they'd already moved on. They were through in the sitting room now.

Bear in mind someone's already reading that paper, Hugh heard himself call. He panicked slightly on the crutches, felt himself sway, righted himself and reached up for the bolt. He slung it home with a manly thud. It was possible Lewis was gay. Certainly Lewis was nothing but trouble. He'd been nothing but taciturn since the old lady. It was something upon which Hugh and his wife, Katharine, whom he loved, were very much in agreement. Hugh manoeuvred himself back into the hall, closed the inner door behind him and swung, with considerable coolness, himself, not an easy feat on a pair of crutches, past the sitting room door.

Doesn't like, he heard Lewis saying, anyone disarranging it before he's read it in the order he always reads it in.

Then the girl's voice; something Hugh didn't catch, because he was clattering through to the kitchen, where Katharine was leaning with her back against the counter doing something on her mobile. She didn't look up.

A child is staying to lunch, apparently, he said.

A what is what? Katharine said. She still didn't look up.

A child, he said. Well, a thirteen year-old. Lewis's friend. Lunch.

Stop making that ridiculous laughing noise, Hugh, Katharine said. It makes you sound insane.

Katharine looked beautiful against the kitchen counter in the spring light. She looked like a disconsolate model from the 1960s as she shrugged and grunted, pocketed her phone.

Ah, Hugh said. Sorry.

I forgive her.

*   *   *

Maybe you'd like to take the hat off while we eat, Ellie, Lewis's mother said to Eleanor Fitzgerald.

Everything meant something else. Lewis knew what this meant: *take the hat off.*

No thanks, Mrs Whittaker, I'm fine, thank you, Eleanor Fitzgerald said.

The way you wear your hat, his father sang.

It meant: *don't worry everything's fine.*

Maybe Ellie is finding it too chilly in here, his mother said to nobody in particular.

It meant: *she better do as I say right now.*

In fact, I'm the exact right temperature, thank you, Eleanor Fitzgerald said.

You won't be able to hear properly with your hat on, his mother said.

It meant: *it's your last chance.*

The way you sip your tea, his father sang.

It meant: *it's all fine.*

Hearing's not a problem, Eleanor Fitzgerald said. If it were, I'd simply have ignored you just then because I wouldn't have been able to hear you.

That would have seemed a bit rude, though, wouldn't it? his mother said.

It meant: *your rudeness has been noted and will be used against you as soon as the correct occasion arises.*

It's philosophically arguable, Mrs Whittaker, Eleanor Fitzgerald said. I mean. Say I don't reply because I don't actually hear you. Does that then make me rude for not replying, I mean in the light of me not knowing I was being spoken to?

The way you answer back, his father sang.

Ali Smith

It meant: *Don't think I'm not paying attention here even if I'm pretending to be likeable and bumbling.*

Ellie is from across the heath, Hugh, his mother said then.

It was a signal to his father that Eleanor Fitzgerald came from the Harper estate. Eleanor Fitzgerald didn't even flinch.

Bet you get a hard time from your friends for wearing that hat in classes, from your peers, his father said. Eh, Ellie? Bet they take you to task for it.

Not really, Mr Whittaker, she said. It doesn't put anybody up or down, really.

And Ellie doesn't eat meat, his mother said.

Course not. Meat's fattening, his father said.

It's actually not to do with any body image propaganda at all, Eleanor Fitzgerald said. It's because of Pythagoras I don't eat meat.

They both stared at her.

Pythagoras is maths, isn't it? his father said.

Eleanor Fitzgerald explained how when she was very young her father had told her about Pythagoras saying that if you kill a cow it's only a very short step from being able to kill another human being.

Dear me! his father said.

It's a nice theory, but I don't think it holds much water in the real world, his mother said.

My father's a commonist, Eleanor Fitzgerald said.

Ah, his mother said.

Lewis saw it cross her face, the moment of her remembering exactly who Eleanor Fitzgerald was.

Well, I hate to be the messenger, his father was saying, I hate to have to report back from history, but you'll have to tell your old Dad that communism's dead and gone, came down in chunks

120

like an old brick wall nearly twenty years ago, will you tell him when you get home? Tell him he'll need a new creed. Actually, capitalism's not doing too well either, eh? We could all do with one. It's Sunday after all. We all need a creed on a Sunday. Eh, Ellie?

Eleanor Fitzgerald shook her head. The earflaps flapped.

No, she said. Commonist. He's a commonist. I'm one too.

Right, his mother said. Interesting.

Commonist, his father said. New one on me.

She told them about how she believed, like her father, in things in common, not just between people but across the species.

That's why I don't eat meat, she said. I believe we have too much in common with other living creatures to eat them.

Then she was off on one, off on her human rights thing. Lewis had read the names on the spines of the books she kept next to the computer in her room. Eleanor Fitzgerald knew by heart whole screeds from their insides. She was quoting now. 'The worst violators of nature and human rights never go to jail. They hold the keys.' That's Galeano, she said.

The fashion designer? his mother said.

The Upside-Down World, Eleanor Fitzgerald said.

It is a bit, isn't it? his mother said. Still, I'm glad politics is coming back into fashion.

Then Eleanor Fitzgerald was telling his parents how the original Magna Carta was written in an ink made of soot and wasp-liquid and tree, how the wasp would inject fluid into a tree when it was laying eggs and then people tapped the fluid out of trees and dyed it to make a kind of ink that would bite into parchment and last for centuries. Lewis had been to see the Magna Carta, or rather *a* Magna Carta, at the British Library across from the Pret a Manger on Euston Road. The one he had seen had been faded and unreadable. It looked like a wiped, flattened stone. It was something about liberty. It was historic.

She was talking about what kind of feather would have been used to write it. A wing feather, from maybe a swan, she was saying.

Would you like to know what happened to my leg, Ellie? his father was saying.

What happened to your leg, Mr Whittaker? Eleanor Fitzgerald asked.

Fell off a swan! his father said. Skydiving!

His father was feeble. His father was like a computer flex that won't fit any of the holes in your computer. He was a redundant flex.

Was whatever really did happen painful, Mr Whittaker? she asked.

Best thing that ever happened to me, his father said. Some things, Ellie, change your life. They really do. Ellie, Ellie, Ellie Fitzgerald. Named after the singer, weren't you, the famous black singer. I'll bet your father's a fan. Bet he wishes he'd something in common with a species of singer as good as she was. I do. I wish I could sing like her. If I were a woman, of course. I don't mean I'd like to be able to sing like her and still be me, or a man. That would be weird, wouldn't it? Or maybe it wouldn't. Would it? What's weird, these days? Eh? Nothing's weird these days, is it?

Lewis looked at his father and knew what love was. It was the terrible knowledge that your father was dial-up in an age of broadband. He looked at his mother. Love was the broken plates of a dinner service, thrown away in a black bin-bag as if the plates had never existed, the breakage had never happened.

Actually, Mr Whittaker, Eleanor Fitzgerald said, though I don't mind you calling me it today because you don't know me, but nobody who really knows me ever calls me Ellie. I was named after my grandmother on my mother's side. She was called Eleanor too, and so was her grandmother, and apparently also her grandmother before that as well. So that if I have a child or children I will ask them to name their daughter, providing they have one, obviously, Eleanor.

Great story, Ellie, his mother said.

Great story, *Eleanor*, Eleanor Fitzgerald said.

His mother raised her eyebrows. *War.*

Lewis, help your friend to more couscous, she said.

I was named, Lewis said, after an island in Scotland they went to on their honeymoon.

It was the first, the only thing he'd said so far. It made his father look pleased (Lewis! his eyes said, though they meant the place, not the son).

I thought you told me you were named after that brilliant old lady who broke out of the hospital before she died, Eleanor Fitzgerald said.

This made his mother shoot him a warning look. The look meant: *don't bring up the Great Aunt Hel thing again Lewis I'm warning you.*

Great Aunt Hel, Lewis said.

Great Aunt Hel, Eleanor Fitzgerald said.

Lewis felt his ears burn with a combination of pleasedness and danger.

We weren't related or anything, he said. She just told me to call her that. She said she liked being called the word great. She lived near us.

Been trying to remember all morning, his father said. The word for when the whole world revolves around the, the, you know, self. What's the word for that? Come on. Three people other than me at this table. Somebody help me.

His father was changing the subject.

Heloise Chaplin no relation is what Great Aunt Hel always said to people when she introduced herself, and when Lewis, when he was small, asked who it was exactly that she wasn't related to, she said *you mean you've never heard of the champ? The kid? The immigrant? The circus? The gold rush? Modern times?* and then, through the letterbox, addressed to Lewis Whittaker, came old film after old film on video and DVD.

She is not related to you, and she is not related to me, his mother had hissed at him in the corridor when he had tried to refuse to come home, when he had wanted to stay overnight at the hospital. She's just a neighbour, she's actually nothing to do with us, his father said when the people at the hospital asked him about funeral costs.

Now she was a name on a plaque on the wall at the Camomile Lawn Remembrance Garden. The name, then the dates, 1918 2008. Her face, kind, old, gone. Nothing and no one would ever be as kind and old again. He had had a stand-up shouting match with his mother and father on the upstairs landing. They said it was because he was spending too much time at the hospital. But beneath it all they were angry at him for not believing what they believed about her.

He didn't. He just didn't, that was all.

For instance: her deaf act proved she wasn't deaf. *I'm sorry?* she'd say first. Then she'd follow I'm sorry with *I beg your pardon?* Then she'd follow I beg your pardon with the single word, like the snap of a gunshot, *what?* and always the same, these same phrases, in this same order, and always with a wink at Lewis because she'd made the person talking at her repeat him or herself.

She could hear Lewis perfectly well.

She'd seen the whole century. She'd taken photos, until she got too old to; they were still somewhere. He intended to find them when he was old enough to find things without having to ask or tell anyone first; photos of history from all over the country, of post boxes near Regent's Park which the historic women blew up and coal miners in their historic battle with the police. It was after he told the story, in the Life Stories module in Citizenship, of knowing Great Aunt Hel, that Eleanor Fitzgerald, who had never spoken to him before, had come up to him after the class and asked what way home did he go and did he want to come over (which had made him feel free as an airborne bird all that afternoon, all that night).

Heloise Chaplin, no relation, walking off down the sunset road to heaven or wherever, a pretty girl on her arm, a little old-lady moustache below her nose. Lewis turned the sludge of pork on his plate over with his knife. He longed to be old and gone. He longed to have seen it all, to be beyond it, to have the right to demand that it repeat itself, explain itself, at his bidding.

So-called incapacitated, so-called demented. She'd disconnected herself (he believed her) from the machine she was wired to, got herself up, past the sleeping nurse and, even though she could hardly walk, into the lift and, when its doors opened down on the ground level, out of the hospital and along the roads by the big houses then down a wet gravel path to a house in darkness, where nobody was home, where she tried its back door and, finding it locked, picked up a geranium in a pot to use the pot to smash a small pane in the door, and there it was, the key, underneath the pot. So she'd had a sleep in a chair in the lounge. When she woke up she locked the house after her and walked back to the hospital, it was five in the morning. She tucked herself back into the bed, reconnecting herself to the monitors, no one even clocking it. *They say it's a medication dream, but I know, Lewis. The smell of geranium. The chair was leather. I held the key in my hand. I put it back under the pot.*

She looked desperate. She had to be believed. It made them furious that he believed her. He didn't know why.

They were both arguing with Eleanor Fitzgerald quite angrily now.

I think you'll find it was after the war, though, wasn't it? his mother was saying.

Which war? Eleanor Fitzgerald said.

The war, his father said. After it the countries all got together and made a declaration.

It was 1998, Eleanor Fitzgerald said. It's a fact. It wasn't made a legality here until two years after I was born.

That's very, very unlikely, his mother said. I think you'll maybe need to check your facts more carefully, Eleanor.

We definitely had human rights here legally before 1998, I'm sure we did, his father said. We're Britain.

The Human Rights Act, which finally made the stuff in the Universal Declaration legal here, was passed in this country in the year 1998, Eleanor Fitzgerald said.

Then she said, Mr Whittaker, what did you read in the paper this morning?

His father's face blanked.

Ah, uh, there was. Lots of things, his father said.

Eleanor Fitzgerald from the wrong side of the heath fixed his parents in her sights above the cooling couscous.

Like what, exactly? she said.

His father looked worried. Then he looked relieved.

Well, money, obviously, he said. Credit, etcetera. And —

something about the Middle East. All the usual. Something about interrogation or moving that prisoner, security stuff. Column about what torture is and what it isn't, legally I mean.

What's torture, Mr Whittaker and what isn't it? Eleanor Fitzgerald asked. Legally, I mean?

I, uh, well, it's. The definition they're giving is there, in the paper. You can read it for yourself. It's through there, his father said.

But you said you just read it this morning, Eleanor Fitzgerald said in her most easy-going voice, the one which filled all the less-good teachers with fear, which was why at school Eleanor Fitzgerald walked the corridors with a golden outline drawn around her.

Tell me a fact, she said now and waited in the silence, in her sheepskin helmet which someone really actually wore to fly in nearly a hundred years ago in the First World War, which until the Second World War happened was known as The Great War.

His father had a line on his forehead. It was made of sweat.

Just one, Mr Whittaker, Eleanor Fitzgerald said. Any single fact that you remember reading in the paper this morning.

I— uh, his father said. Uh—.

His mother interrupted.

What was that thing, Hugh, you told me this morning, about violins, she said.

His mother pinked, looked sheepish. His father looked astonished.

Yes, his father said. Violins. Wait. The really old kind, they're one of, of, the only things in the world that never lose their true monetary value in an economic downturn. No matter how bad the downturn. There, Ellie. How's that for a fact? Eh?

He saw the look pass between his parents.

It meant: *gotcha*.

*   *   *

Truth be told, I did feel a little guilty about it, Hugh Whittaker told his wife, whom he loved, from bed that night.

Katharine had her back to him. She wouldn't come to bed. She was on her laptop at her dressing table, not speaking, making little noises when her fingers hit the keys.

I mean about the violin thing, Hugh said.

The violin thing had been in the paper several weeks ago, not today at all.

But he had wanted, himself, to pull that leather cap off the little girl's head and throw it across the room. Just to show her. It was laughable, to be lectured by a child, that a child could sit there and act like she knew more than you did with such, what was the word, again? Impecunity. Katharine had told him afterwards who the little girl was. The school-run grapevine report was that she'd been in trouble with the police, taken down to the station and given a dressing-down, for taking photographs of policemen.

Really? Hugh said.

Uh huh, Katharine said.

So it's another batty old lady thing with Lewis, then, the little girlfriend? Hugh said.

Maybe, Katharine had said. I hadn't thought of that. It's possible. He's deep, Lewis. He's original. I think, in reality, he's grieving for himself.

Of course, she was right. Definitely. You had to admire Lewis; it had certainly been a very original way to disturb your parents, an infatuation with a mad old urine-smelling woman who acted like everything was being stolen from her regardless of how nice you tried to be to her. Self-indulgent adolescent grief took courage. He'd said it again: *you're right about everything.*

Am I? Katharine said.

Yes! Hugh said. He'd laughed. Then he'd apologised for laughing. Katharine hadn't noticed. And since we're talking rights and wrongs, she'd said. When did it become wrong?

I don't follow you, Hugh said.

Is it? Katharine said.

What? Hugh said.

Wrong, Katharine said. To take photographs. Just take photographs. Of policemen. Is it against the law? When did it become against the law?

Absolutely no idea, Hugh said.

So if you or I went out with a little Kodak, Katharine said, like the one I had when I was a child, and we took a photo of a policeman, we'd be breaking a law?

Before they'd married she had told him she liked his laugh, that it made her feel safe, like nothing could possibly go wrong.

She was still sitting there making the little noises. Snap snappity snap snap snappity.

God, Katharine said.

She closed the lid of the laptop. She muttered something under her breath.

What? Hugh said.

Everything that girl said, she said.

Sorry? Hugh said.

True, Katharine said.

Katharine left the room. He heard her go through to Lewis's room. Then he heard her go downstairs, he heard the front doors opening one after the other. He listened for the noise of shutting. It never came.

He reached for the crutch, got himself out of the bed.

By the time he got to the window and pulled the blind up she was stomping over the heath. She was still in her nightclothes.

She never went walking on the heath. She was phobic about dogs' mess. He knew her. She'd simply never.

She was completely gone. He couldn't see her at all.

When Lewis woke it was to his mother shaking his shoulder. She was saying something. Tuung was still playing in his ears. *Woodcat o woodcat. And we all had a lovely time.* He took one earphone out.

Your friend, his mother said. Her address.

Why? Lewis said.

Tell me, his mother said.

It meant: *tell me.*

He told her. She left the room, dressing gown flying. Lewis sat up, dazed. He heard the door open, then the outside door.

His mother had cracked.

Eleanor Fitzgerald's house would be in darkness. Her father was on nightshift. She stayed with her mother on Sundays.

He would get up and find his trainers. He'd set his mobile to the torch setting. It was dark on the heath.

He'd go downstairs and out the open front doors. He'd walk past Great Aunt Hel's house. There were new people in it now.

By the time he'd get to Eleanor Fitzgerald's street, his father miles behind them both, negotiating the first potholes and clumps at the edge of the heath with the tips of his crutches, Lewis would see his mother at the door. He'd hear the faraway doorbell sound repeat. He'd watch her step back, stand in the street, strain to see in the upstairs windows. She'd be imagining Eleanor Fitzgerald in bed asleep, still wearing her flying helmet.

When he'd get close to its front gate he'd hear her, his mother. She'd be broken and kind, down on her knees shouting words through the letterbox into the empty house.

So much, his mother would be calling. Common. Please. Forgive.

RODDY LUMSDEN

Now based in London, Roddy Lumsden was born in 1966 in St Andrews, was a student at the University of Edinburgh and is a former vice chairman of the Poetry Society. His first book, *Yeah Yeah Yeah* (1997), was shortlisted for the Forward Poetry Prize (in the Best First Collection category). Subsequent collected works include: *The Book of Love* (2000) – a Poetry Book Society Choice and shortlisted for the T. S. Eliot Prize and the John Llewellyn Rhys Prize; *Roddy Lumsden is Dead* (2001) and *Mischief Night: New and Selected Poems* (2004), which *Scotland on Sunday* described as being 'as raw and self-lacerating as Berryman, as wry and self-deprecating as Morrissey'.

Lumsden's most recently published collection is *Third Wish Wasted* (2009) and, for the independent poetry publisher tall-lighthouse, he is currently editing the *pilot* series of chapbooks featuring eighteen poets under the age of thirty.

In addition to poetry, and teaching at London's City University and Morley College, Lumsden has also written *Vitamin Q: a Temple of Trivia Lists and Curious Words* (2004) which reflects another parallel career as a puzzle-setter and quiz writer, notably for BBC *MindGames* magazine.

THROUGH A RAISED GLASS

Roddy Lumsden

One thousand thank yous, poet, for telling me
about my own people, for instructing me
in the anthropology of ruder ways
and simplest faiths. I am richer now for gazing
at your word-paintings of the ungrandeur
of the schemes, the base calm of terraces
which hide stout garden sheds scented with
Maxwell House and thinners, where stony men
suck smokes and spin the handle of their vice,
rolled-up tabloids jammed into the rule sleeve
of their overalls. I had never before noticed
the dods of dog dirt on the black bags piled
behind the one-room library, the sick mist
rolling between tower blocks; I was blind
to frozen food palaces on two-Greggs-streets,
bowling halls and bowling greens and bowl-cut

kids whose only sports, I see now, are daydreams
and venom. Had you not veered into the badlands
en route to your office at the end of a corridor,
your cafetière, your modest photocopy budget,
had you not rummaged through the crumpled snaps
of the relatives your family rarely mention,
had you foresworn that commission at the prison
which funded the long weekend in Salamanca,
I would be still be miscuing, hitting the wire,
sending the rain-soaked ball over the crossbar
of the truth, my education being comprehensive
only in name. I would barely recognise myself.

ANDREW CRUMEY

Author, schoolteacher and post-doctoral research associate – he has a PhD in theoretical physics from Imperial College, London: these are just a few of the strings to Andrew Crumey's bow. Born in Glasgow in 1961, he grew up in Kirkintilloch, attended the University of St Andrews and, ultimately, settled in Newcastle upon Tyne.

Published in March 2008, Crumey's most recent novel, *Sputnik Caledonia* has been shortlisted for the James Tait Black Memorial Award: coupled with his previous success as an author, it was this book when still a work-in-progress which won him the £60,000 Northern Rock Foundation Writers' Award in 2006 and enabled him to concentrate full-time on writing. In its review, *Scotland on Sunday* said, 'The sweep and scope of *Sputnik Caledonia* should leave you breathless with admiration: not only do we learn, as we often have from Crumey's novels before, but we also laugh, a lot. *Sputnik Caledonia* is a quantum leap forward for the Scottish novel.'

135

Crumey's debut novel *Music, in a Foreign Language* (1994) won the Saltire First Book Award and his subsequent novels have garnered critical acclaim: *Pfitz* (1995), *D'Alembert's Principle* (1996) *Mr Mee* (2000) and *Mobius Dick* (2004). He was selected as one of *Granta*'s Best Young British Novelists, but disqualified himself by pointing out he was a year older than their limit.

THE LAST MIDGIE
ON EARTH

Andrew Crumey

I was on a gap year before beginning my degree in celebrity studies;
I packed a few clothes, beach-wear, my battered old guitar, and
flew to Scotland where I'd never been but had often dreamed of.
I'd seen a picture in a book when I was a kid, long sandy beach,
waves breaking gently, one or two bathers. This was Scotland: a
peaceful, unhurried place where life was easy. There was that movie
about the guys who ran a little tavern, they'd sit around staring
at blue sky from under their broad hats, dreaming, philosophising,
falling in love. Sure, I wanted some of that northern bliss, being
able to stay outside nearly all of the day and never burning too
much, even with only low-factor protection. I wanted to strum
my guitar and hear cicadas chirping, watch pelicans alight on shore-
side gantries.

I decided I'd get myself to an island called A-Ran, heard it
was good for full-moon parties. First ride I hitched was in a
sugar-truck, couldn't believe they still ran those things, must

have been a hundred years old. Driver was called Dizzee and smelled of bacon, took one look at me, heard my accent and said, 'Welcome tae God's own country.' I liked that. They're such religious people.

Dizzee had this little thing hanging inside the cab of the sugar-truck, dangling over the control board, not much bigger than my thumb, kind of a geodesic shape with black pentagons on it so I figured it must be like an icon or something. He said it was called a football: you touch it for luck. Dizzee told me about his two wives and six kids, he was about seventy, I think, though it was impossible to guess his age, the climate's easy on these people, they pick fruit the whole year round. Dizzee was delivering a consignment of kyleberries and not in any hurry. The spoiled ones had been juiced to power his truck.

'Where I come from, they banned these things a long time ago,' I told him.

'It's these things gave us all the life we got now,' he said.

'How's that?'

'Carbon.'

He told me this long and important story I forget, too busy looking through the cracked side window at the scenery slipping past. Whitewashed houses with their windows flung open to greet the balmy air; old ladies on rickety chairs gossiping cheerfully outside brightly painted front doors. A tavern whose sheltered terrace seemed an island of calm within calm.

Something else went by. 'What's that?' I asked.

'Grass.'

'What for?'

'Football. Needs a lot of watering though.'

I twisted to watch the retreating rectangle of yellow-green and thought of all the holy services that must go on there, people on their knees bowing east or west or whatever they do, wearing their traditional tartan bonnets.

'You a student?' he asked.

'Sure.'

'How come you're on your own?'

I had to think about it. 'Better travelling alone.'

His stubbly chin curved into a wry smile. 'Just you and your guitar, eh? That's nice. Expect you're looking for some female company, though. Not that I'm presuming, mind.'

I felt embarrassed but reminded myself these are passionate people, openhearted, frank. They live outdoors, baring their skin to the not-too-hostile sun. I'd even heard they made love on their roof terraces. Well, it was in that movie.

'So what's your place like, son? For girls, I mean.'

I told him how we all mostly have to stay covered up so it's sometimes hard to tell the difference.

'Aye, I've heard about that. Suppose it could add to the excitement though.'

I thought of telling him about 27, my girlfriend. I could show him the picture on my memory card, the one she zoned when we met on the interpoint. I thought of the voice of her text and wondered if we'd ever get to meet each other in ambient space, wondered what it must be like to live wholly in flesh and blood, like these people, not digitally enhanced. My world was artificial and theirs was real. While I thought all this, Dizzee kept talking.

'Stanley Baxter . . . Robert Burns.' He was giving me a history lesson. 'Fafnir Trolsdottir . . . Manjit Raj.'

I don't think I'd heard of any of them but I could see that Dizzee took it all very seriously. Mostly they were poets, philosophers, revolutionaries, I think. Also one or two chefs.

'I saw the movie about those guys opening a tavern,' I said.

Andrew Crumey

He glanced at me with playful scorn, then indulgent pity.

'Aye, that. It was OK, I suppose. But the Chinese always get Scotland wrong.'

Dizzee drove me to a town called Krankie where our routes diverged. He dropped me at the town square, place like something from a storybook, a real open-air paved area with a fountain in the middle and short-sleeved people strolling. There were tottering infants, geriatrics walking arm-in-arm, and wherever I looked my eyes couldn't help falling on the slim, gently tanned legs of tall, exotic girls.

'Giesa a chune then.'

I turned and saw one standing right next to me, less than an arm's-length away. I instinctively backed off and put my hand over my mouth.

'Ah'll no bite ye!'

I reminded myself I wasn't in the Dome now: there were no viruses to worry about here, only food poisoning and malaria if I didn't maintain standard precautions. She nodded at the guitar neck protruding behind my shoulder.

'Ur ye gonnae play that thing or is it just for show?'

I pulled it round in front of me and strummed a chord. 'I need to tune it . . .'

'Aw, don't be shy. Bet you're dead good.'

Her voice, strange and melodious, was like primal music, wholly natural and infinitely mysterious. She was pretty as a ripe tomato. I played *Peace Song of the United Workers*.

'No bad, that. Catchy.' She said it as a way of making me stop. 'I'm March.'

'Hello, March.'

'You'll never guess what month ma burthday's in.'

'Won't I?'

140

'Wannae meet ma pals?'

She pointed to a café terrace at the other side of the square where a large group sat round two or three tables, everyone gesticulating and talking at once, the way they do. I followed her there, a couple of them looking round when we arrived and March introduced me.

'This is— Whiss yer name?'

'Kalo'

'This is Carlo and he's gonnae play a chune for us.'

A few more broke away from their conversations, sipping chilled bubblegum lattes while I began reprising *Peace Song of the United Workers*.

A dark-skinned girl asked, 'Zat a hit where you come frae?'

I nodded.

'Know any we'd know?'

She suggested a few titles that must have been religious songs. Seems they do a lot of singing at the football.

'Moan an sit here wi me,' she ordered, but March wasn't having it.

'He's mine!' she laughed.

I'd been in Krankie all of ten minutes and here were two beautiful girls fighting over me. I wish 27 could see this, I said to myself. Wish everyone in the Dome could see. In the end I sat between them, once some people had swapped places to accommodate. The other girl was called Purple; she pointed to a muscly guy with a bandana at the far end of the group and said he was her boyfriend, I didn't catch his name but he smiled hello. Purple said he was a health consultant in the evenings and a gym instructor by day. I'd thought all these people were farmers and fishermen or tourist industry workers but I suppose you've got to have other jobs to make an economy work. They all kept talking about money.

'Thing is,' Purple explained, 'we're a poor country, backward, been like that for decades, centuries, whitever. So we've got tae work hard if we're gonnae catch up wi the likes o yous.'

March agreed. 'Post-colonic, that's whit we are.'

Purple told me about her cousin who emigrated. 'He wis in that dome o yours, cleaning supervisor, fourteen-hour shifts every day, made a packet, sent it all back here tae his family. Now they've got a big place on A-Ran.'

'I'm heading there.'

'Y'are? Look him up – ah'll gie you his contact.'

'You mean it?'

'Seriously. Tell him ah sent ye.'

'You're not just saying it? Where I come from, when you give someone a contact and tell them to get in touch, you don't really expect them to show up at the door.'

'Aye, well, we're different. Here you go.'

She brought out her mem-card and flashed the details to mine, then scrolled up a picture of her cousin's island home. 'Look at that, no bad, eh?' A sprawling villa with an arcaded portico. 'They've got horses and everything. He's loaded.'

'All from working as a cleaning supervisor in the Dome?'

'Och no, it's from the business he started efter he came back.'

March butted in. 'He's a gangster.'

'No he's no!' They both laughed but I couldn't tell how close the joke was to the truth: in this country everything was done with bribes and kickbacks, that was what I'd heard. It was in that movie. Only way they could open the tavern was by settling things with the local mob.

'How ye getting to A-Ran?' March asked.

'Hitching.'

'On a copter? Jetfoil?'

'Could always swim there,' Purple chuckled.

'Ma dad knows this skipper,' said March. 'He'll gie ye a lift.'

A few texts were enough to settle it, though not on the sugar-boat she'd thought, instead a hoverboard taking oranges and a few tourists later that day. There was space for me too if I didn't mind standing.

'You're all such kind people,' I said. The hours slipped like sand.

It worked out just as March promised: the hoverboard was bumpy but it felt good to be so close to the gentle sea, watching endless whitecaps and the occasional rise of dolphins. One kid swore she saw a flying fish while her mother unwrapped sandwiches in the salty air whose tang on my parched lips was like a kiss. A-Ran rose through heat haze but by the time we shored the sun had dipped behind mountains and a welcome coolness had arrived. At the quayside I stopped to look at a shrine to a famous ancient poet called C. John Taylor who summed up the spiritual effect of so much natural beauty in a verse I can't remember except for the last line: '*It's nice to be nice*'.

There was an old woman in a bikini with a beach towel round her waist, plump and sun-leathered, sunglasses perched on her head. I showed her the house I was looking for on my mem-card and she recognised it at once, nodding with appreciation. 'The big fella, eh?' Everyone on the island knew Purple's cousin. 'Moan and ah'll show ye.' She led me along the esplanade, sandals flapping on the warm asphalt, and when eventually she paused I thought it was to admire the pelican we saw squatting on a capstan being fed sardines from a bucket by two small children. In fact she wanted to point out the hilltop overlooking the sea where the villa stood. 'Ten-minute walk,' she informed me, and in her bluntness I noticed for the first time the pride that for these Scottish people lies just beneath the simple friendliness. It made me suddenly aware that she was old enough to be my grandmother yet was wearing what in the Dome would not even count as underwear.

Time means nothing to them – the ten-minute walk was more like twenty. But eventually I reached the villa, looking just like the image I had of it except for a new extension on one side. Fixed to the gate was a neatly made sign: Big Fella.

I walked up the path and rang the bell, a dog barked inside, nobody came. I rang again and the barking was joined by gruff shouts; I saw through the frosted door-pane a large approaching figure and when he opened up I found myself looking at Big Fella himself, unshaved, in a string vest and with a drink tin in his hand. He stared suspiciously while I explained myself, but as soon as I mentioned Purple he smiled broadly and welcomed me inside, taking me to a spacious marble-floored room hung with abstract oil paintings. He said they were by his wife. The Scots are highly artistic people.

In the Dome you only ever make contact by appointment but straight away this man was treating me like part of the family, inviting me to sit down, wanting to know all about me, and about the Dome he hadn't been to in years, asking when I'd be going back, and if I wouldn't mind taking a package for him as long as it wasn't too much trouble.

'What sort of business do you do, Mr Fella?'

'Import and export,' he told me.

'Anything in particular?'

'This'n'that.'

I found myself staring at the large canvas hanging behind him, a lot of dark blue with streaks of red that looked like they might be part of someone's anatomy. It made me think of those beaches I'd heard of where they don't even wear swim-suits, only sun-cream.

'Fancy a beer?'

I didn't know what he meant at first, then worked out he was offering me the same kind of traditional beverage that was in his hand. He went to fetch me one and I looked at more of the paintings. They all had those splodges and swirls that looked vaguely rude. Big Fella's wife was obviously very talented.

He came back and handed me a chilled tin but it was such an old-fashioned kind I didn't even know how to open it. He helped me crack the lid and a button of foam spat out.

'Cheers, pal.'

'Thank you, sir.' It tasted disgusting, like mouldy bread. I guessed they didn't put sweeteners in their drinks because they needed all the sugar for their transportation vehicles. 'You mentioned a parcel . . .'

'It's nothing, son. Friend of mine's needing some medicine, that's all.' There were rules and regulations, apparently, stupid laws that meant he couldn't post it. 'Like the pictures, eh? That wee one there's a cracker.'

'Is your wife a professional?'

'Ye could say that.'

I sipped the beer as slowly and politely as I could, wondering what it was made from. In the movie they only ever drank stuff called wine that was really grape juice, they pressed it themselves from the fruit of their own vines. But the Chinese always get Scotland wrong, I'd discovered. In reality those grapes would more likely power a smoke-belching hoverboard. Beer must be a way of recycling bakery by-products. Might even have some kind of religious significance.

He told me he was a collector, pointed to a cabinet in a corner of the room and we went to look at what was inside: old coins and credit cards, a printed circuit, a bag made of polythene. His home was stylishly uncluttered, but a few ancient objects, carefully placed and thoughtfully displayed, created an air of taste and beauty. He showed me an antique device called an iPod, with parts a person would put inside their ears. Something to do with telepathy or mood control, I think, and although it obviously no longer worked, he still wanted me to try. I thought of all the infectious agents that could have accumulated on those porous buds over the years and politely said no. In another part of the room stood an archaic microwave oven that still pinged, and near it on a plinth I saw Big Fella's most precious relic, a glass box whose tiny occupant was held on a gold pin I could barely bring into focus beneath my eyes. Big Fella supplied a magnifying glass. It was, he said, the last midgie on Earth.

'Ye'll be stopping wi us after the party won't you?'

I hadn't known about it, but Big Fella said there was a full moon – I was in luck. He insisted I stay. That was one thing the movie certainly got right: the kindness and generosity of these people.

'Nother beer?'

I'd drunk hardly any: Big Fella suggested I might like to try a different beverage and brought out something called whisky. It looked promising because the measure he poured was a lot less than what was in my beer tin, though when I tasted it I could see why. I believe they make it by steeping chillies in oil for several years. Big Fella suggested adding water and in this way I was able to drink quite a lot, being thirsty from the long day's heat.

I started to feel dizzy. Perhaps I'd picked up something blown from those ear buds because really I wasn't right at all though I didn't want to say anything to Big Fella who was being so friendly. What happened during the next few hours is not completely clear. At some point his wife Angelica arrived, blonde and beautiful and many years younger than Big Fella. She wanted to hear me play guitar so I suppose I must have sung *Peace Song of the United Workers* while she sketched my portrait in charcoals. When she was done she turned her drawing board and showed me what she had seen: a pile of geometric shapes in need of shaking. I think the next thing that happened was she started taking off some of her clothes.

Suddenly there were other people, many of them, and we were all on the beach standing naked beneath the bright round moon. There was some woman doing a lot of shouting who taught degree courses in shamanic drumming. And we burned a dead dog, or perhaps I only imagined that part. Well, here I was in the land of love and peace, the place I'd come in search of, even better than the movie about the guys opening a tavern. Everybody gets Scotland wrong, they think of beaches and hydrosurfing and don't realise it's a state of mind, it's about having the freedom to discover who you really are. Big Fella took me to one side and started explaining about the parcel, only some white powder in a little plastic bag for his sick friend, though on account of those stupid rules and regulations I'd need to hide it in an unusual place if that was OK, not the sort of place I'd ever thought of putting anything at all but a natural pocket of sorts, I suppose. And I said sure, no problem, because Scotland is a land of spiritual freedom and in Scotland nobody says no to anything, only an everlasting yes, in fact they were all shouting it in unison while that woman was banging away at her drum: 'Yea! Yea! Yea!' But Big Fella must have detected a flicker of doubt because he said to me, are you really sure? You won't go telling anyone? He got Mrs Fella to contribute to the discussion and she was pretty persuasive. And all the time I kept hearing the shouts of the revellers, seeing their beautiful moonlit bodies. Never anything like that in the movie, I can tell you.

A very long time ago, maybe hundreds or thousands of years,

I don't know exactly, midgies were these creatures that gave you plague and made Scotland a miserable unhappy place of war and famine. Kind of a symbol you could say, symbol of a nation that was sick and needed healing. But now the midgies were gone, and here were all these joyful, welcoming people, cured and free, and it was places like my own that were sick, the Dome, with its endless artificial daylight and sanitised air. 'You need tae live a little,' Big Fella advised. And you know, that is so profound. It's like in Scotland everyone's a philosopher, everyone's a poet. So let's do it, I thought. Let's live a little. Because when you really get down to it, it's nice to be nice.

JOHN BURNSIDE

Prize-winning poet, writer of short stories and novelist, John Burnside was born in Dunfermline in 1955 and grew up in Corby, Northamptonshire. He studied English and European languages at Cambridge College of Arts and Technology and worked as a computer software engineer before becoming a full-time writer in 1996. Formerly a writer in residence at the University of Dundee, he now lives in Fife and teaches at the University of St Andrews.

Burnside has won the Whitbread Prize for his poetry collection, *The Asylum Dance* (2000), the Encore Award for his prose, *The Mercy Boys* (1999) and the Saltire Society's Scottish Book of the Year Award for his memoir, *A Lie About My Father* (2006). His collection of short stories, *Burning Elvis*, was published in 2000 and his novels include *The Dumb House* (1997), *Living Nowhere* (2003), *The Devil's Footprints* (2007) – shortlisted for the 2008 James Tait Black Memorial Prize (for fiction) – and *Glister* (2008). His *Selected Poems* were published in 2006, with subsequent

John Burnside

collections, *Gift Songs* and *The Hunt in the Forest*, appearing in 2007 and 2009 respectively.

Of his work, *Scotland on Sunday* said, 'Burnside writes with an almost preternatural acuity . . . He is perhaps one of the only living poets who can use words such as "sacred" and "holy" in an unironic manner . . . He has gone on to write works in which unexpected epiphanies and reconciliation are as thrilling, haunting and provocative as violence and horror.'

THE FAIR CHASE

John Burnside

De torrente in via bibet;
propterea exaltabit caput

Psalm 109

What we were after there, in the horn and vellum
shadows of the wood behind our house,
I never knew.

At times, it felt like bliss, at times
a run of musk and terror, gone to ground
in broken wisps of ceresin and chrism,

but now and then, the beast was almost there,
glimpsed through the trees,
or lifting its head from a stream

John Burnside

to make us out:
a coarseness on the wind
and brittle voices sifted from the morning.

We tracked the scent through barley fields and hollows,
we followed it into the spinney
with billhooks and sickles,

but nothing was ever there, save the codling moon
and, far in the meadows,
the one field of nothing but grasses

where something had lain,
in a fetor of blood-warmth and pollen,
before it moved on.

Still, we continued;
when one man sickened and died,
another would take his place in the wandering column,

blacksmiths and lawyers, orchardmen,
butchers in waiting,
lost in the fog, or hallowing after the pack,

and all of them friends of my father's; though, needless to say,
in a country like this, the dead have more friends
than the living.

We were the men you saw
on a winter's morning:
cumbersome bodies, shrouded in gunsmoke and cyan,

we went out every day, in every season,
falconers, rat-catchers, deerstalkers, whippers-in,
plucking at shadows, purblind, afraid of our dogs,

and if, on occasion, I never quite saw the point,
I was always the first to arrive, with my father's gun,
bound to the old ways, lost in a hand-me-down greatcoat

and last among equals – flycatcher, dreamer, dolt,
companion to no one,
alone in a havoc of signs.

*

One year, the reservoir froze.
I walked out to the centre of the ice
and gazed down through a maze of gills and weed

to where a god I'd read about in books
– sweeter than pine, but stone-hard in his tomb –
lay waiting for a gaze to curse with knowledge.

The ice was clear as glass: I hunkered in
and dared him, from that unreflecting world,
to pull me through, in one bright flash of rage,

no crack, no sudden drop into the cold,
nothing to witness,
nothing to remember.

John Burnside

Minutes I waited; then the others came
and called me back, the dogs a swarm of noise
and worry, old men's

faces in a mist of their own breath
ashamed for my father's sake
and his father before him.

We carried on; I walked off to one side,
and halfway through the white of afternoon,
I slipped away, unwanted, or unnoticed,

taking a road less-travelled through fields and yards
of stunted brassicas and rotting tyres,
strangers in coveralls or leather aprons

stopping to watch as I passed: no hand raised in greeting,
no dog come out
to see me on my way.

That was a foreign country: snowdrifts, then sand,
blotted and kissed with yew-drupes
and windfall holly,

spotted owls hunting for beetles along the hedge,
smoke in the distance, nether roads,
passing bells.

I walked for hours, yet it was light as noon
when I came to a place I thought I had seen before
through a lull in the weather:

nothing to speak of,
a dirt track and sheep in the woods,
and that sense of a burial, under the moss and ruin,

but something was present a few steps into the tree line,
one of those creatures you find in a children's album,
a phantom thing, betrayed by smoke or rain,

or glimpsed through a gap in the fog, not quite discerned,
not quite discernible: a mouth, then eyes,
then nothing.

It lingered a while;
and then, as if it wanted me to play,
it shifted away through the trees – and I followed after.

Crashing through cover, ducking through sumac and maple
it leapt and ran, though never so fast or so far
that I couldn't keep pace

and when I paused for breath, it also paused
and stayed,
as if it wanted me to follow.

I never saw it clear, but it was there:
sometimes the brown of a roe-deer, sometimes
silver, like a flight of ptarmigan,

it shifted and flickered away
in the year's last light
and I came after, with my heavy gun,

John Burnside

trudging for miles
through meadows laced with rime,
working by scent

and instinct, finally
true to myself,
with the body and mind of a hunter

and, by the time I stepped into a glade
candy-striped with light and frosted grass,
I knew exactly what a man should do

in my position – lucky, singled out
by death and beauty for the blessed kill,
assenting to the creature's dumb assent

to blood and darkness
and the life
beyond.

I took a bullet,
loaded it with care
and aimed with an intent that felt like love

– though I only knew love
by hearsay
and stubborn lack.

No sound, no movement; all the world was still
and not a creature in it
but ourselves,

me taking aim
and the animal stopped in its tracks,
waiting to see what would happen, unafraid,

a deer, I thought, and then I saw a fox,
and thinking I knew what it was
I pulled the trigger.

The old days were better for mourning;
better for tongue-tacked women
in ruined plaid

climbing a hillside
to gather the rainwashed bones
of what they had lost, that winter, to the cold,

and men in the prime of their lives,
with dwindled sight,
dreaming all night of that slow white out by the river

where, once or twice a year,
a girl would drown,
pledging her heart to a boy she had mostly imagined.

I remembered the flow country, then,
as the gunsmoke darkened:
I'd go there as a child on Sabbath days,

my father asleep in his church clothes, a fret of chickens
wandering back and forth
at the kitchen door,

John Burnside

a lull in the house and that emptiness high in the roof
as if someone had frittered away
in a summer wind.

I'd go out in my Sunday clothes and shoes
to the shimmer and dart
of sticklebacks threading the light

and search for something I could never name,
the blue of a smile, or the curious
pleasure of the doomed, as they go under;

and that was what I hurried out to see,
crossing the space
to where the beast went down

but all I could find when I got there, standing dismayed
in the stopped air of afternoon, with smoke on my lips
and my heart like a fettered thrush in the well of my throat,

all I could find was an inkwash of blear in the grass
like the fogged stain after a thaw,
and a ribbon of musk

threading away to the trees
and the distance beyond:
no body, no warmth, no aftermath, nothing to prize,

and the night coming down all at once,
like a weight at my shoulders,
settling in waves, till all I could see was my hands.

Everyone becomes
the thing he kills
– or so the children whisper, when they crush

a beetle or a crane fly in the dust,
feeling the snuff of it bleed
through the grain of their fingers;

I'd always thought of that
as superstition:
a wishful thinking, how the spirit moves

from one shape to the next
like breath,
or warmth,

infinite kinship, laid down in the blood
against the sway
of accident and weather;

yet out in the woods that night, as I dug myself in
to wait for the day, I felt it in my gut,
a gravity I'd never known before

dragging me down
so it seemed I would cleave to the earth,
the life I had taken

snug as a second skin.
I should have died, if not for that faint warmth
that held me there, unseeing, in a night

John Burnside

so utter, dawn
was like a miracle:
the trees emerging, piecemeal, from the cold,

a snowflake here, then there, then everything
arriving all at once, as I awoke
and, never having slept, began to walk.

I didn't know how far I was from home,
but nothing looked familiar
– not the woods

and not the road I found that afternoon,
dizzy from cold and hunger, hurrying on
through empty yards and desolate plantation,

nothing alive
as far as the eye could see,
only the white of the sky, like a wondering gaze

pursuing me from one field to the next,
from ditch to ditch,
from wall to broken wall.

I walked like that for days. The road led on
through spruce and lodgepole pine, then dipped away
to where a village lay, warmed in a crook

of hills that seemed familiar, suddenly:
a spill of lights and woodsmoke and a church
that made me think of something in a book

before I made it out. My dead were there
among the tilted stones;
I knew the market cross; I knew the spire;

but everything was strange, even the house
I came to at the far end of the lane
that passed the abattoir then crossed the brook

and finished at the unclipped cypress hedge
where no one lived next door,
through there were ghosts,

so frail, I only knew them by the sound
the wind made
when it worried at the shutters.

Nobody lives
here now, it's only
crows and bees

and every shift
and slant
is an event

historic
in its void
of mud and wire.

Yet now and again
I have turned
in a falling shadow

John Burnside

and caught a glimpse
of something
at my back,

not heard, or seen,
but felt,
the way some distant

shiver in the barley registers,
before I can think to say
it was never there.

The hunters pass at daybreak, casting
curious looks at my door, but no one is here
to see, as they go to the woods

and disappear.
Nobody lives here now, not even me,
and yet the house is mine – a net of dreams

and phantoms
where that cunning animal
I followed through the woods sits in my skull

and calls out for the life it must have had
in the green of the trees and the absolute white of the snow,
where I am hunting, hunting even now,

hearing that call,
and turning around
for the echo.

JAMES ROBERTSON

Born in Kent in 1958, raised in Stirlingshire, a student at the University of Edinburgh and now living in Angus, James Robertson – poet, novelist, short story writer and editor – writes in both English and Scots and, as general editor of the Itchy Coo imprint, has produced many Scots language titles for younger readers, including translations of Roald Dahl and A. A. Milne.

History, politics, language and culture number among Robertson's particular interests and inform his adult fiction: *The Fanatic* (2000), *Joseph Knight* (2004) and *The Testament of Gideon Mack* (2007) – which was long-listed for the Man Booker Prize. *The Testament of Gideon Mack* was described by *Scotland on Sunday* as 'a fabulous fable, encapsulating the last fifty years of Scottish history while simultaneously being a parable about redemption, judgement and fidelity.'

Robertson's poetry includes translations of Charles Baudelaire and Dugald Buchanan and a verse sequence on Alfred Hitchcock.

James Robertson

He has also edited the *Dictionary of Scottish Quotations* and the anthologies *A Tongue in Yer Heid* and *The Smoky Smirr o Rain*. In 2004, he became the first writer in residence at the Scottish Parliament, a position which led to a collection of essays and poems entitled *Voyages of Intent*.

MACTAGGART'S SHED

James Robertson

That morning, before it was fully light, before he had drunk a cup of coffee, even before the first whisky of the day, Christie saw ghosts crawling through the field opposite his house. He had come to in the armchair in the living room. He wasn't sure what had woken him. Probably a tractor or car going by. His head ached and his mouth felt like it was stuffed with newspaper. The room was still half-dark and he stumbled over an empty bottle lying on the carpet as he went to the window and pulled back the shabby brown curtain.

Across the narrow road was the big field, and beyond it another road, and beyond that trees and more fields rising up into the hills. There were houses dotted along the distant road and also on the hillside. He could see lights in some of the windows, but it was not yet bright enough to make out smoke coming from the lums. He remembered the smoke that had poured from those houses when they'd been set on fire. He remembered their neat red roofs before the fighting started and later, when the fires were out, the charred rafters through which could be seen the raging green of abandoned gardens. A few of the houses had been repaired since then, by men who had brought their families from other villages and settled into them as if they owned them. Those were the ones with lights showing. But most remained broken and empty, reminders of what had happened. It was as he was thinking this that something caught his eye in the big field and he saw the ghosts.

They were moving with painful slowness through the shaws of MacTaggart's winter crop, from which strips of mist were hanging like tattered flags. Christie watched as the ghosts crept across his vision, from right to left, away from the end of the field where MacTaggart's old shed had been. He should have been filled with horror but he was not, he felt only a dull stirring of the old fear that had been with him for months. It was as if he had been expecting them. He'd not known he was expecting them, but as soon as he recognised what they were it made sense that they were there, and that they were on their hands and knees trying to get away from the shed.

The crop was Brussels sprouts, a vegetable he hated, and the shaws were like miniature versions of those stark, blasted trees that appeared in photographs of the trenches in the Great War. The ghosts might have been the ghosts of soldiers crawling in no-man's-land, but they weren't. There seemed to be a lot of them, far more than there should have been. Christie tried to count them but they were indistinct, and low on the ground. He could hardly make them out at all. He wondered if the dog would have a ghost and tried to pick it out among the shapes, but then they all started to look like dogs. After a few minutes he could not concentrate any more, and went to the back of the house, to the kitchen.

The kitchen window looked out on his scrap of back yard which ended at a listing wooden fence. Beyond the fence was a dirty wee burn. A couple of starlings were pecking at the hard soil of the yard where he sometimes flung out the crumbs of an old loaf. Christie preferred the wee, bonnie birds – chaffinches and robins and blue tits: starlings were too ragged and sly and oily-looking to be bonnie, but at least they were real. His hand shook as he filled the kettle and put a spoonful of coffee grains into a mug. When the water had boiled he poured it into the mug. He liked his coffee black and strong. He added a shot of whisky from the bottle that was standing on the worktop next to the cooker. The bottle was almost empty. He wondered when Malky would come.

The kitchen was cold. The whole house was cold. The fire in the living-room had died in the night and he would have to reset it later. The television was also dead but it had been dead a long time. He did not remember falling asleep but there was a book crushed between the cushion and one arm of the chair and he guessed he had gone under while reading it. He took his coffee through to the bedroom, slopping some of it on the floor as he went. He did not have any shoes on, and there were holes in his socks. He did not take off his socks nor indeed any of his clothes as he got beneath the covers. None of these things was surprising or unusual to him. The ghosts were unusual, he had never seen ghosts before, but even they were not surprising.

By the time he had drunk the coffee, his hand had stopped trembling. He did not know, nor did he care, whether this was due to the whisky or because he had warmed up under the bedclothes. He thought vaguely about going back to the kitchen for the rest of the bottle but he felt a vague, distant comfort from being in bed. It reminded him of being ill as a child, of the security of being in a sick-bed. He snuggled down and pulled the blankets over his head. In a minute he fell asleep.

He had redd out the cold ashes from the hearth and was just putting a match to the re-laid fire when he heard Malky's motor pull up. Christie recognised the sound of its exhaust, the way it coughed and hacked like a smoker. Malky got out and slammed the door shut, leaving the engine running as he always did. Christie heard the front door bang. Malky came into the room with a large carrier bag in his hand, which Christie tried not to look at.

'Aye, Christie. How are ye the day?'

'I'm fine,' Christie said.

'Just up, are ye?'

'Aye.'

They stood together and watched the flames lick up the paper and the kindling begin to crackle.

'Ye'll need tae pit some coal on that,' Malky said. 'Dae ye hae plenty coal, Christie?'

'The bunker's still hauf full,' Christie said. 'Ye ken that.'

'I just wouldna want ye tae be short. I can get ye mair when ye need it. Here, I've brocht ye a few things tae keep the wolf fae the door.'

He put the carrier bag on the carpet in front of the fire. It was a plain blue bag, its handles stretched by the weight of its contents. Malky began to empty it.

'Some breid,' he said. 'Bacon. A dozen eggs. Four cans o beans. Ye can mak a few meals oot o thon. And here's somethin tae wet yer whistle wi.' He took out two bottles of Whyte & Mackay.

'Ye shouldna hae done that,' Christie said.

Malky said, 'Ach well. They were on special offer for twa. Keep ye oot o danger, eh?'

'Keep *you* oot o danger, mair like,' Christie said, trembling at his own boldness.

'Now, now, Christie,' Malky said. His black moustache seemed to thicken and bristle up. 'Dinna start. I'm just tryin tae help.'

'Aye, I appreciate it.'

'Gillian's askin for ye.'

'She awright?'

'Right as rain. She's no gaun oot muckle these days, though. Like yersel. It's no the season for it.'

'Naebody gaes oot ony mair,' Christie said. He knew this to be the case, but it wasn't because of the time of year. The road outside went to the village and yet there were never more than a dozen vehicles on it all day. As for walkers, there were none at all. Auld Sammy used to take his dog along to MacTaggart's farm and back every afternoon. But he wouldn't be seeing Auld Sammy again.

'She's feart,' Christie said. 'Like me, right enough. She's feart.'

Malky snorted. 'Naw she's no. She just hates this time o the year. Cauld, dreich, dark. *I* wouldna gae oot if I didna hae tae. She keeps hersel busy, but. She's aye cleanin and cookin, cleanin and cookin. A right wee domestic goddess.'

Malky moved to the window and stood with his back to Christie. *I could lift the poker and crush his heid wi a single blow*, Christie thought. But he couldn't. The poker was a feeble thin thing, not like the old heavy-duty ones. And he wasn't strong enough. Malky was built like a house-end, he wouldn't even dent.

'MacTaggart's pit his sheep intae the field, I see,' Malky said. 'It's a shame tae see aw thae sprouts away for sheep feed. Still, canna be helped. Naebody tae lift them.' He turned. 'I never really liked sprouts onywey. Do you, Christie?'

'Naw,' said Christie. He wanted Malky to fuck off, but he didn't tell him. Malky was his brother-in-law. And he had brought the food and drink, after all. He was always bringing things. Just about every single day. And he never asked for money. It wasn't about money.

Malky didn't seem to know where to put himself. His bulk took up half the room. He picked up a cushion from the second armchair, turned it over, patted it and put it back. He shook his head.

'Christ, ye're a manky bastard. This place is a cowp.'

'That's how I like it.'

'And what aboot that television? It's years since that worked. I can get ye a new ane. Or a good quality second-hand ane at least.'

'Aye, so ye keep tellin me. But I dinna want a new ane. That ane suits me fine.'

'But it disna work!' Malky sounded exasperated, but Christie knew what he was playing at. If he got him a new television, that would be another distraction. Another way of controlling him, like the whisky. But he'd finished with the television – had left it on day and night till the back of it melted – and one day soon he'd be quitting the whisky, but not yet. At least with the whisky he could think his own thoughts.

'Dae ye no want me tae get a woman in tae gie the hoose a good clean?' Malky said. 'Gillian'll ken somebody.'

'Can ye she no come hersel?'

'Aw, noo, Christie, ye ken she canna. She's no weel. She's nae energy. Canna dae the hoosework like she used tae.'

Christie knew he was lying. He'd just left off calling her a domestic goddess. Gillian was stuck in the house for the same reason Christie was: fear. And Malky wouldn't let them meet. His own sister. Not without him being present. If they met they'd start talking. Spilling the beans. *And mair than four fuckin cans o them tae.* Those international guys that were supposed to be snooping about, asking questions. Malky didn't want Gillian and Christie getting any ideas about speaking to *them.*

Outside they heard the car engine splutter and die.

'Fuck it,' Malky said, 'I'd better go. I've got frozen food in the boot.'

'Aye, right,' Christie said. 'Thanks for coming by. Wi thon stuff. I can drink mysel tae death in comfort.'

Malky laughed uneasily. 'I think ye'd hae done that by noo if ye were gaun tae.'

'Well, the gas oven then,' Christie said. He had a wee smile in his chest but he kept it off his face. He liked to goad Malky. 'Or the razor blades. *Schff, schff!*' He made cutting noises and swift cutting motions across his wrists.

'Dinna talk like that, eh?' Malky said. 'That's no nice. I'm keepin an eye on ye, amn't I? Ye're awright, eh? Ye wouldna dae onythin stupit, would ye.'

The last sentence was more of a statement, or a threat, than a question. Christie knew Malky wasn't talking about suicide. Malky was worried about him going to the police. Not the local mob, worse than bloody gangsters they were. The international boys.

'Or the shotgun,' Christie added. 'I could stick the shotgun in my gub.'

Malky snapped. He towered up, heaving like a bull, and pulled Christie in close by a fistful of jersey. Christie could hear teeth grind. He'd got to him.

'That's enough,' Malky growled. 'Stop feeling fuckin sorry for yersel. Jesus, when ye think o aw the folk in the world wi – wi nuthin. *You're* awright. D'ye hear me? Ye're *awright.*'

He let go, and Christie, looking down at his chest, saw the

clump of jersey spring open. He found that strangely more interesting than looking at Malky.

'And ye dinna hae a shotgun,' Malky was saying, more gently,
as if to a forgetful child. 'We took it away fae ye, mind?'

Christie did not answer. 'Suit yersel,' Malky said after a minute.
He banged out of the house. As he got into the car he shouted,
'I'll be back the morn, see if ye're mair fuckin sociable.'

Christie grinned and punched a fist into his palm. He loved it
when he put one over on Malky. Fact was, he had another shotgun.
Up in the loft. And a full cartridge belt. And a whole box of grenades.
And an AK-47 and an automatic pistol. He had the lot. Keeping them
for when he needed them. But because he was just a school janitor
– had once been a school janitor – nobody took him seriously when
it came to that kind of stuff. Nobody believed him. And the international guys wouldn't believe him either, not just him on his own.
He needed more witnesses. He needed Gillian. Gillian must have
seen the state of Malky's clothes. She must have washed and dried
them. Maybe she'd burnt them. But she knew. She had to know.

The only thing anybody'd ever believed him about was the way
the bairns behaved in school. The *other* bairns. In the corridors
and in the playground. They liked to hear him go on about that.
*The wee tykes. The dirty wee shites. The thieving, treacherous wee
bastards.* And they'd laugh and come up with their own stories.
Everybody had them, it only took someone to start it off and you
were all away. The teachers were the same. Our kids and their
kids. You could tell them apart just by looking at them. By their
names. By the state of their clothes and the food they ate. Some
teachers claimed they could pick them out by smell if they were
blindfolded. It was probably true. Christie didn't like them any
more than anyone else. And that was just the bairns. The bairns
grew into adults and then the trouble really started.

He went to the window and looked across at the field. There were twenty or thirty sheep in it right enough. He might have mistaken them in the half-light of early morning. But that didn't mean the ghosts weren't there. He'd seen them, crawling away from where the shed had been. MacTaggart's brick shed with the corrugated iron roof where he'd once kept an old tractor and trailer. All gone now. Malky had made MacTaggart pull it down. 'Take away the shed,' he'd said, 'and it'll be like nothing happened.' You had to have a scene for something to have happened. Now there was just Brussels sprouts, getting eaten by sheep.

MacTaggart was a nasty piece of work, Christie thought. He used to claim that Auld Sammy only went to the farm to steal tatties. Sammy went up with his dog and an empty plastic poke and came back with enough tatties to feed his family for a fortnight, so MacTaggart said. Finally he'd threatened Sammy with his shotgun, told him not to show his dirty face near the farm again. A nicer old fellow than Sammy you couldn't meet, even if he was a minker and a thief. Always passed the time of day. And the scabby dog was friendly too. Not that Christie would ever have had them in the house, because they weren't his people, but that wasn't the point.

When the fighting started, the school closed and Christie was laid off. It was only supposed to be temporary till the unrest died down, but it didn't, it got worse. You didn't realise till it started how many of the bastards there were. There had always been a kind of undercurrent that boiled up every so often in pub brawls, graffiti sprayed on shop fronts, vandalised cars, but then something changed, people stopped backing down or holding back and it all just escalated. Folk had always gone on about the numbers, how they were going to take over if something wasn't done about it, but it wasn't till you saw them with guns and your own people with guns that you got a real sense that it might actually happen. The bairns had mixed pretty well on the whole, forby a bit of name-calling and a few scraps among the boys, but when everybody retreated into their own houses that was the end of any mixing. Christie lay awake at night and heard pick-up trucks roar past that he knew were full of armed young men. He heard shots at three in the morning, explosions. He looked out into the darkness and saw the houses on the hillside ablaze. In order to sleep, he drank more and more whisky. But when he slept he dreamed. In his dreams he saw the bairns from the school playground running screaming down the road. He couldn't tell which bairns they were. They were like the bairns in the old photographs from Vietnam, their naked skin burning with napalm. In order to stop dreaming, he sat up in his armchair and watched television, and drank till he did not so much fall asleep as fall unconscious.

Malky used to drop in at odd times of the day and night then. He'd wake Christie up if he was sleeping, and they'd sit drinking together: beer, whisky, wine, whatever Malky had with him. He always had drink and he always had money. He talked about the night rides, the gun battles in the towns. He talked about the women they took into the woods and what they did to them. Sometimes they didn't even bother taking them into the woods. Christie listened and he imagined what it would be like. He'd brought his father's old shotgun down from the attic when the fighting started, and kept it handy just in case, because you never knew when somebody was going to come to your door, and sometimes when Malky was talking Christie'd take the gun out of its case and oil it, clean the barrels and look down them as if he knew what he was aiming at. He'd just be cleaning the gun while Malky was talking, that was all. Like a couple of solid guys going about their business.

Standing up for what was theirs, for their rights. Christie wasn't stupid. He reckoned there were two reasons why Malky came, and why he talked. The first was that he needed to tell someone, and he couldn't tell Gillian. The second was that he knew Christie wanted to hear.

'I'd take ye,' Malky said, 'but they wouldna allow it. Ye kinda hae tae pass a test. They hae tae ken ye're no gaun tae fuck up.'

'I wouldna fuck up,' Christie said. 'Honest.'

'I believe ye,' Malky said. 'But no everybody does.'

'Who? Who d'ye mean? Folk in the village?'

'Some. They ken what ye're like. And then there's the others, the boys runnin the show. They wouldna allow it.'

It was all shite really. Christie didn't want to go and Malky didn't want to take him. But it was okay talking about it, listening to what Malky was up to. Listening made Christie feel like he could do it if he had to. And it was good drinking with somebody instead of on your own, even if it was just Malky.

Then one morning – a morning when there had already been a lot of traffic up and down the road, which had got Christie out of his bed early – Malky rolled up in his coughing car with two other men in the back seat. Christie went out to meet him – in those days he still used to step outside. Malky said, 'The bastards've done it this time. They've killt young Jock MacTaggart. They're roundin them up noo.' Somebody had tried to set fire to MacTaggart's place in the night, and when the MacTaggarts came out fighting whoever it was had shot the farmer's son through the head. Whoever it was! They had fled the scene, but MacTaggart, the old bugger, he knew fine who they were.

'So,' Malky said, 'are ye comin?'

'Me?' Christie said.

'Aye. Come on. I've spoken for ye. 'This is Christie,' Malky said to the men in the back seat. 'My wife's brither. Mind I said aboot him.'

The men in the back seat didn't reply. They were wearing dark glasses and black leather jackets and they were very calm.

Malky seemed agitated. 'Come on, then, Christie,' he said. 'We're maybe ower late as it is.'

Christie went back into the house and got the old shotgun and slung the cartridge belt over his shoulder. He climbed into the front passenger seat and they drove off towards MacTaggart's place. But they hadn't gone more than a hundred yards before they saw a strange procession coming down the road towards them.

There was a pick-up at the front and MacTaggart, in his Massey Ferguson, was herding the procession from the back. MacTaggart's face was like a concrete slab, hard and empty. There were men with guns on either side of the procession. They'd got twelve of them: six men, four women and a couple of bairns. The women were sobbing, and the bairns were sobbing because the women were. The six men, who were all at least fifty, looked quite calm, but it was a different kind of calm from the way the men in the back seat looked. More placid than calm. One of the men on the road was Auld Sammy. He had his dog on a lead, and he appeared to be humming a tune.

Malky reversed the car up onto the pavement and switched off the engine. Usually he left it running but this time he switched it off.

'It canna hae been them. Can it?' Christie said.

'Fuckin right it can,' one of the men in the back seat said. Christie turned round. The one who had spoken had a ring in his right ear. Neither of them was from the village.

'But that's Sammy,' Christie said.

The car filled suddenly with silence.

'Who are you?' Christie asked after a few seconds.

'Fucksake, Christie,' Malky said. 'Ye dinna need tae fuckin ken that.'

'I'm just askin,' Christie said. But he turned round and faced the front again.

'Is he wi us or no?' the man with the earring said.

'He's wi us,' Malky said.

'Cause if he's no wi us, he's wi them,' the man said.

'Christie?' Malky said. He stared right into him.

'I'm wi you,' Christie told Malky.

'Right,' the man with the earring said. 'Nae mair fuckin questions then.'

They all got out. The procession turned into the field and the pick-up pulled over. Now MacTaggart was revving his tractor, urging the people on across the drills towards the shed. Some of them stumbled and the women cried louder. Malky said, 'Aye, ye can greet noo, ye thievin hoors,' and he sounded bolder than he was looking and Christie laughed. Auld Sammy must have heard them because he turned to say something and one of the armed men beside him prodded him in the side with his rifle and he fell to the wet earth. The man kicked him to make him stand up and Christie wanted Sammy to get to his feet and he wanted him to stay where he was. Sammy's dog was running round in small circles trailing its lead, barking and snapping at the legs of the man standing over Sammy. The man pointed his rifle at it and Sammy raised his head and called to the dog and it came and sat beside him. The man pointed his rifle back at Sammy.

There seemed to be a moment when everything might be different. Everybody – the men with guns, their prisoners, MacTaggart in his tractor – stopped and watched Sammy. Even the two men in leather jackets and dark glasses hesitated. It was as if somebody, with some brave, simple gesture, could change whatever was going to happen. And Christie thought, *I can dae something here, I can really dae something.*

Then Sammy caught sight of Christie and seemed to recognise him for the first time. His eyes flickered with uncertainty. He looked at Christie's face and then he looked at Christie's shotgun. There was a long streak of mud down Sammy's clothes where he had fallen on the ground. It made him look even more of a minker than usual. Christie kept his eye on the streak of mud. That way he thought he could do what he was going to do.

'Wait!' he shouted. He was calling to the man pointing his rifle at Sammy's chest. Christie walked over with the shotgun cradled in his arm, right past the man with the rifle, and helped Sammy to his feet. He felt big and powerful, like a man in a film.

'It's awright, Sammy,' he said.

He took the end of the lead and together Sammy and he started walking towards the shed with the dog between them, and everybody else started moving too. Sammy started to hum again. Up close it was a completely tuneless sound, more of a moan or a whine than a hum. Christie hated it, he wanted Sammy to shut up so he could concentrate. Something big was coming, something so big you needed to focus all your thoughts on it and not be distracted. Christie felt as though by being there some great mystery was about to be revealed to him. It was like a Bible story from when you were a bairn, a story that you believed but didn't understand, and now suddenly, years later, you were about to understand it. And these people, these miserable people moaning and girning the way they always did, they were the key to the mystery. And the mystery was in MacTaggart's shed.

But when they got to the shed Christie didn't go in. MacTaggart stopped his tractor and got down and pulled open the sliding door with a blank expression on his face, as if he might be going to fetch a couple of sacks of fertiliser or something but didn't really care one way or the other if there was none there. They ushered the prisoners towards the door. Auld Sammy looked at Christie and he started to shout, he was shouting, 'Help us! Help us! Why are ye just standin there? Help us!' The man with the earring was watching intently. He didn't seem to see Sammy any more: he was staring at Christie to see what he would do. To see if he would fuck up.

Christie was still holding the dog's lead. He said, 'I'll tak care o yer dog.' Sammy shook his head. Christie said, 'Sit!' and the dog sat down beside him. Then they pushed Sammy and the rest of them inside the shed and the other men, including Malky and MacTaggart, went in too. The only ones who were left outside were Christie and the man with the earring.

There was a sudden clatter of gunfire from inside the shed, and then nothing.

The man with the earring said, 'Nice work, Christie. But ye canna keep the dog.'

'How no?' Christie said. He searched for the man's eyes behind the glasses, but he couldn't see them.

Malky came out of the shed. His clothes were spotted with blood and so were his hands. His face was very white.

'He canna keep the dog,' the man with the earring said. 'Tell him.'

'But I said I would,' Christie began, and Malky's face flushed up red and he bore down on him so close he could smell the blood on his shirt. 'Ye canna keep the fuckin dog!' Malky said. He flicked his eyes indicating the shed behind him. Christie could hear teeth grind. Auld Sammy's dog was sitting patiently waiting for Auld Sammy to come out. Christie realised that what they were saying was right. He couldn't keep the dog. He pushed the barrels of the shotgun gently against the back of its head, shut his eyes and pulled both triggers.

'Put it inside,' Christie heard the man with the earring say. 'Ye can clear up later.' He kept his eyes closed and stood absolutely still, and he heard heavy breathing around him and wondered what would happen next. He knew with absolute certainty that he could not go into the shed. The only way they'd get him in there would be if they carried him.

A few seconds went by, and each one felt like a minute. Then he heard someone bend down next to him, and give a groan with the effort of lifting something heavy, and when he opened his eyes he saw Malky's gun on the ground and Malky's back as he carried the dead dog into the shed.

Malky came into the house later that day and the first thing he did was punch Christie in the face, sending him crashing into his armchair. Christie sat rubbing his jaw but he didn't get back up, he knew why Malky had done it. Malky took a new bottle of whisky out of a plastic bag and cracked the top open.

'Ye stupit fuckin eejit,' Malky said. 'Ye're lucky tae be alive. Ye dinna mess aroond wi thae guys. Get us some glesses.'

So they sat drinking, and Christie rubbed his jaw and started to talk about what had happened, just the way Malky used to talk about his night rides, but Malky interrupted him.

'Forget it, Christie,' he said. 'Forget it all. Forget aboot Sammy and the dog and everything ye fuckin saw. It didna happen. Awright? It didna fuckin happen.'

And that was the way it had gone on. MacTaggart pulled down the shed and there was nothing inside it and then he planted Brussels sprouts all over the field. Malky would come round and make sure

Christie had food and drink, and Christie would try to talk about what had happened and Malky would tell him to forget it. 'Ye're imaginin it, Christie. Ye've been watchin too much shite on the telly. Aw thae news programmes ye watch, the documentaries and aw that. That aw happens somewhere else. Other countries. No here. Ye're away wi the fairies.'

'But I seen ye comin oot the shed,' Christie would say. 'We took Auld Sammy and them inside and ye came oot wi blood on yer claes. I was there, I'm a witness. And I killt thon dog wi my faither's shotgun,' he would say.

'Christie, Christie, ye're makin it up. Ye're no right in the heid. That's why we took the gun aff ye. That stuff's aw aff the telly, Christie. It's got inside yer heid fae the telly.'

'Ye didna tak the telly aff me, though, did ye?' Christie said. He kept quiet about the stash of weapons in the attic. Let them have the shotgun if it made them feel safe. He had another. Plus the other stuff. A whole bloody arsenal.

'Didna need tae,' Malky said. 'Ye knackered it wi leavin it on aw the time. But I can get ye another ane if ye want. Ye ken that.'

'Naw,' Christie said. 'That ane suits me fine.'

The truth was, he didn't need the television. He looked at the stuff Malky had brought, still sitting on the carpet in front of the fire. He didn't need the bread – the starlings could have it. He didn't need the eggs or the bacon or the baked beans. He looked at the whisky. He didn't even need the whisky, but he needed to think, and the whisky would help him to think. He needed to make a plan. He had to get in touch with Gillian somehow. He had to get in touch with the international boys, tell them about what had happened in the shed. He was a witness. All right, he had shot the dog, but only the dog, and he'd had no choice, they'd have killed him if he hadn't. He picked up the coal hod and shoved more coals on the fire. He remembered the houses burning on the hillside. Terrible, terrible things had happened. He felt numb with the thought of all that hurt. He went to the window and looked out. It would be getting dark again soon. He wondered if he would see the ghosts again, and how many there would be. He reached for the first bottle of whisky, and started to plan what he would do in the morning.

JAMES KELMAN

With the novel set in his Glasgow homeland, *How late it was, how late* (1994) James Kelman became the only Scottish novelist to date to have won the Booker Prize. Indeed, since his short story collection *Greyhound for Breakfast* won the Cheltenham Prize in 1987, Kelman has picked up a steady stream of awards and nominations including: the James Tait Black Memorial Prize (for fiction) and a place on the Booker shortlist for *A Disaffection* (1989); the *Scotland on Sunday*/Glenfiddich Spirit of Scotland Award plus the Stakis Prize for Scottish Writer of the Year for the short story collection *The Good Times* (1998) and the Saltire Society Scottish Book of the Year Award, the Aye Write Bank of Scotland Prize and a Scottish Mutual Investment Trust/Scottish Arts Council Book of the Year Award for *Kieron Smith, boy* (2008). He was also the sole UK nominee for the 2009 International Man Booker.

Other titles by the author include short story collections such as *An Old Pub Near The Angel* (1973), *Not not while the Giro* (1983)

James Kelman

and *The Burn* (1992); the novels *The Busconductor Hines* (1984), *A Chancer* (1985), *Translated Accounts* (2001) and *You Have to be Careful in the Land of the Free* (2004); the essay collection "*And the Judges said . . .*" (2002) and many plays for radio and stage.

TALKING ABOUT MY WIFE

James Kelman

I should have been working or else calling into the pub for a couple of pints before the last stretch home. I sometimes did that coming off the nightshift on Friday mornings. Even if I was working an overtime shift into Saturday, I still liked that Friday morning. There was a pub near the Cross that opened for breakfast. A couple of us went in there. We did not stay long, an hour or so, three or four pints. The lasses were well away to school by the time I strolled home and Cath would be up and about, giving me looks.

Anyway, she had been asleep when I opened the door. So how come I was home like this? I saw the question. She was frowning and blinking at the alarm clock on the dressing table. Dont worry, I said, it's no time to get up yet.

She turned her head from me, her eyes closed. She aye had difficulty getting out of bed. I had difficulty getting in it.

I leaned across to her, laying my hand on her thigh. She screwed up her eyes, gave a slight shudder instead of a smile, then her exaggerated shiver; she should have had that copyrighted – or copywritten, whatever you say.

She lay further down, pulling over the quilt and snuggling in. I grinned. She was more awake now, squinting at me which meant I was to speak. Explain yourself man! I might have smiled.

My presence at such an ungodly hour! I could only shrug and tell her the truth, an approximation to the truth. I had a fall out with the gaffer, there was a bit of bother. Other women might have accepted that. Cath was not other women, and her silence continued. Are you going back to sleep? I said.

She ignored this. What does 'ignored' mean? I do not know. I have to be honest, I was rather weary. I sat down on the bedside chair and unknotted my shoe laces. Oh dear, the shoes. She hated me wearing shoes in the house, especially the bedroom, but anyplace where bare feet were liable to tread. Our lasses had pals and when they brought them into the house they forgot to tell them to take off their shoes. This drove Cath nuts. I did not blame her but it caused emotional mayhem in the highways and byways of our apartment. Then again the lasses did not like telling their pals to take off their shoes. It made them seem stupid, that was what they said.

Oh Mum nobody else does it.

I dont care what nobody else does.

But they tell people in school and they laugh at us!

I stayed out it. Domestic issues are an awkward reality. Very much so in our house.

What I was thinking was get my own shoes off and a quick wash and into bed. Tomorrow is a brand new day. Except literally it was not. It was the exact same day as here and now. It was Friday morning and would be Friday dinnertime when I arose Sir Frederick, arise ye and walk the plank ere doom befal ye.

Man, what a life.

She lowered the quilt to beneath her boobs. I was about to say something further but the mammarian physicality beat me. I reached to hold her hand instead. But even that was off-putting. Cath's hand is a really sort of pleasant thing, it is soft and warm. I always found it pleasing in an aesthetic way. I used to like drawing when I was a boy, I would have drawn her hand. Her fingers were long and seemed to taper, and then if she had a varnish on her nails. It just looked good. Had I been that way inclined I would have varnished my nails.

And what do I mean 'that way inclined'! So now when I looked at her, with silly thoughts crossing my mind, I could only smile and this made her suspicious. So how are *you* doing? I said. Did *you* sleep?

She did not answer. I was suddenly tired, most tired, needing to stretch out beside her on the bed here and now, right here and now. I took off my second shoe but continued sitting there. And a song went through my mind. My little nephew sang it to me a week past and it went something like:

I'm so silly
silly silly silly

Me and him sang it walking up and down the hallway like a pair of demented soldiers:

I'm so silly
silly silly silly.

I would like to have done it with the gaffer. That bastard. I would have goose-stepped him along the factory floor, Groucho Marx and Ginger Rogers:

> *I'm so silly*
> *silly silly silly.*

Aw well. And my neck. Interesting to note that I had developed a nervous condition on the right side of my neck; it entered spasms at the slightest emotional activity in one's brain-box. All soldiers are demented. All professional ones anyway. Every time I hear one talking I want to have their parents arrested for child abuse. I mean ordinary soldiers, not these upper-class fuckers who march them as to war.

I sighed, I was enjoying the seat. So: this was Cath I was talking to. Well well well.

The truth is me and her were incompatible. On occasion. Was this such an occasion! I guffawed inwardly, and needed to sneeze immediately, grabbed for a tissue from her side of the bed, and gave the snout a hearty blow. I think there is something wrong with my nose, I said.

Oh that is interesting, muttered one's missis.

What is that new-fangled expression, 'pear-shaped'? I think it might describe my life.

So what happens now? she said.

In what respect I thought but said nothing. What happens now? Worth pondering. What does 'what' mean? Even before getting to 'now' that statement was beyond my intellectual capacity. 'Happens' is just a verb, which makes comprehension easy. With verbs concepts are straightforward, it is the actual doing that causes trouble, translating into action, getting from concept to movement.

Man, how many pints did I not have? This is the last time I would forego my Friday morning breakfast booze-up.

But I felt like a sandwich, a bit of toast or something.

Cath sighed. I sighed as well. But her sighs were significant. Mine were just sighs.

Fucked again I thought, but in what way? I did not answer the sigh lest incriminated. Except when Cath sighs one is required to answer. What is troubling you madame?

No, I did not say that. I did not, in nowise, say that. Fear. Not in so many words. Nor was I sure what to say. I got up from the chair and walked to the window, parted the curtains a little. Your Honour, I cannot deny that that is what occurred on the morning of the fourteenth.

Maybe she wanted a cup of teh. Her pronunciation of this aye reminded me of her granny, a lass from Mayo whom I met and loved for one week in the merry month of July, during my courtship of the illustrious Catrine her granddaughter.

I was about to ask if she wanted a cup but she spoke first. Do you mean you have got the sack?

Of course not!

Of course not? Did I actually say that? What a fucking liar man! I would have burst out laughing except she was staring at me, staring me down. I had been about to look out the window. Now I felt like a total tube, like a naughty boy, I said, caught in the act. That is what I feel like.

So what is it? she said. What happened? Was it a fall-out? What actually happened? Do you really mean you got the sack?

I smiled. You are some woman, telling you, the way ye say stuff.

So you have not been sacked?

Sacked! Even the word sounds strange to the ear, to my ear

anyway. When the hell was I ever sacked? Have I ever been sacked?
I cannot remember. I do not think I was ever sacked, not in my
whole life.

'Sacked'. There is something anti-human about that term. I do
not care for it. Here you are as an adult human being, a thinking
being to use the ppolitical terminology, and then you are to be
'sacked', this canvas bag is to be pulled over you, hiding you
completely. None can see one. Then one is smuggled publicly
from the place of one's employment, in the erstwhile sense.

Sacked, I said, what a word!

Cath looked into my eyes with a steady gaze, her sparkling blue
eyes shining as befits a latter-day femme fatale, one who is given
to ascertaining the thoughts of a mancub by return so-to-speak,
in other words, as soon as one has the thoughts they are tran-
scribed into her nut.

I hope this makes sense, I said, what happened apparently is
that I was sacked.

She wanted further information. Her continued silence indicated that. The truth is she was an innocent. There are a lot of
women like Cath. They know nothing. Cath knew nothing. She
had never experienced the actuality of work. Genuine work. Jobs
where things like 'angry gaffer' and 'sack' crop up regularly. In
her whole life she had never worked in an ordinary hourly paid
job. Office stuff was all she did. That was a thing about women,
they were all middle class. She knew nothing about real life, the
kind of job where if ye told a gaffer to eff off you collect yer
cards at the end of the week. That was power and that was power-
lessness.

Would you like a slice of toast? I said.

She did not answer. Other matters were of moment, weightier
than toast.

No they were not. Come on, I said, let us have a bit of toast, a cup of tea.

Cath studied me. This was no time for toast and tea. Life was too important. Seriously, I said, I am not powerless, I have it in me to act and here I am not so much acting as in action, I am making toast and tea.

Cath did not smile. My attitude is more being than assumption of such. She knows this and does not care for it. When we were winching, back in the good old days when choice was probable

I lost that train of thought.

Here is the reality: I was an ordinary worker. Power there is none. It did not matter I was a would-be author on matters cultural, ppolitical and historical, to wit my life. None of that mattered. I existed in the world of 'angry gaffers', data such as 'sack' and other matters of fact.

Man, I was fucking sick of it. And having to please everybody. That was part of it. That was an essential part of it. Then coming home here and having to do the same in one's domestic life. It was so fucking— oh man

Sorry Cath, what did you say? the thought returneth.

I didnt say anything.

I thought you did. Because there is no point attacking me like it is my fault, it is not my fault.

I didnt say anything.

I am glad because really

I did not say anything.

Right.

I am not attacking you.

Okay then but in a sense you are, your manner. It is like you are blaming me. That is like what you are doing. You dont say anything except just look but you do look, you look at me, and it means things that are mentally uncomfortable, psychologically I should say.

I beg your pardon? Cath almost smiled.

You're blaming me without even knowing the circumstances.

I'm not.

I think you are, you have been. I'm sorry, if I jumped the gun, I'm sorry.

Cath sniffed softly, continued to study me. She was no longer lying on her back: I should have pointed this out. By now she had raised herself onto her elbows then plumped up a pillow and squeezed it behind her shoulders, and propped herself against the headboard. She did all of that while I was blethering like a dang-blasted nincompoop. Her arms lay in a natural damn position across her lap which lay concealed beneath the quilt. Mind you,

no, forget that.

Cath was entitled to stare at me and stare she did. And I was entitled to ask why. There are no bones to be picked.

What are you talking about?

I shrugged, coughed to clear my throat.

Did he honestly sack you?

No, I said, not at all.

Honestly?

Honestly.

She shook her head. An instant prior to that I realised that my lies were no good: my lies never had been: my lies were of the load-of-shite variety, only fit for a barrel of keech; to have been dropped into such. She said, Oh well, you can always get another one. You're always saying it's a rotten job. So, ye can get another one.

Oh yeh . . .

You always say you can.

Sure. Jobs dont grow on bushes, but I can always get one.

She drew the cardigan across her shoulders. Can I talk to you or not?

I wasnt being sarcastic.

Cath nodded.

I wasnt.

Sorry, she said. Now she smiled but it occurred to me that the way to describe this smile was 'sad', she 'smiled sadly'.

No, I said, I'm sorry.

I dont know what to say.

There is nothing to say. I raised my eyebrows and scratched my head in a gesture that used to make her smile, reminding her not so much of Laurel and Hardy but the skinny half of the duo, for I, dear reader, am a wee skinny bastard.

What? said Cath.

I shall just have to apologise to the shit, the gaffer.

She smiled.

Honestly. I said, That is what I'll do, I'll walk in tonight and I shall go up and see him immediately. Excuse me, I shall say, and he shall look at me and . . .

It was difficult to utter the next bit because no next bit existed. Cath was waiting.

I should apologise, I said, really, because it was me that was out of order. I attacked him in front of other people. Like a humiliation nearly. He would have regarded it as such.

Oh.

I sat on the edge of the bed, reached for her hand, stared into the palm holding the edge of the tips of her beautiful fingers. I shall tell you your fortune, oh mistress of mine, oh mistress of the flowers, you shall go on a long voyage, you shall be accompanied by a small balding stranger who is

You are not balding.

Yes I am, face it, I refer here to your husband, to wit, myself.

She laughed lightly but was worried. She squeezed my hand. You dont tell fortunes in the right hand, that's the one you are born with.

Honestly?

Yeh.

I stared into her right palm, now her left, compared the two. Well well well, I said, and I aye thought they were the same. So, perchance, this explains the ill winds that blow always in my direction.

Cath smiled.

The truth is . . . I half smiled.

What? she said.

I dont think I can handle working these days my dear. It is all just cowards and bullies. One is surrounded by them. Ye cannay even talk in case it gets reported.

They wont all be like that.

Nearly. Times have changed. I cannot talk to these blokes, I cannay actually talk to them. Except about football maybe, I can join in then, fucking football. I closed my eyes, speaking rapidly: Sometimes I want to do him damage. I'm talking physical stuff like battering him across the skull, that is what I'm talking about, dirty evil bastard – telling ye Cath I'm working away and my head's full of scenarios, I'll be down the stores and way at the back and he comes along, he doesnt know I'm there, I hide behind the stacks of platforms, then when he appears I jump out and smack, across the back of the skull, a shifting spanner or something, a big file maybe, I hit him with it, crunch.

That is horrible.

I smiled.

It's the way animals behave.

I nodded.

You wouldnt stoop to that?

Not at all, I said, and couldnay hide the grin which must have lit up my entire fizzog as they say in US detective stories. But that is how it gets ye and ye wind up as cowardly as the rest of them, little shit that he is – I mean metaphorically – he is not little at all. Nowadays ye do not get little gaffers. Physical intimidation is part of the job. Honest. I dont even think he is a coward. They say bullies are cowards at heart. I'm unconvinced by that. I think we just like to think it is the case, it cheers us up. I hate even looking at the guy, if he is talking to me, I cannot bear it, honestly, I cannay; I just cannay fucking bear it. It is like I might vomit over him as we converse.

Physical intimidation! I wish he would try that, I said, fucking ratbag, then we would find out. Seriously though, I am going to take him on. This time he is not getting away with it.

I stopped, the way Cath was looking at me.

I know what ye're thinking, I said.

Then I'll not say it.

I nodded, studying the lines in the palm of her hand. Abracabranksi!

I said that to make her smile. I used it with my lasses when they were wee. That is the one magic word above all. Abracabranski. The lasses thought I was kidding. But I wasnt, like the best magic it was secret; nobody else knew it, just us, us.

Cath was unsmiling. Yes, she said, I shall say it, because I have to. Why does it have to be you? Why does it have to be you? Are you the only one? Why is it you? Why does it have to be you?

Why does what have to be me?

You know what.

I dont.

She stared at me.

I dont. I dont. Eh . . .

Why are ye smiling?

Smiling?

But I had smiled. What she said was true. Even as we spoke I was smiling. Two reasons: 1) She thought nice things about me concerning the opposite of moral cowardice 2) She performed a movement of her shoulders that was characteristic. Naybody else in the whole world did it. Except her granny. But she had died ten years back. Cath was alone. Unless the lasses maintained the tradition. Still and all I found it weird how this one solitary manoeuvre might force me into saying things I did not want to say. I refer to commitments. I did not want to commit myself to a single damn thing!

What is it? she said.

What is what?

You shook your head.

Oh did I?

She sighed.

Cath, it doesnay matter.

What doesnt.

I unclasped my wristwatch, laid it on the mantelpiece. I reached to switch on the radio but paused, and asked first. Mind if I put on the radio?

I would prefer if ye didnt.

Aw.

If ye dont mind.

Of course.

I'm going to lie down, she said.

She had taken the cardigan from her shoulders, she laid it along the foot of the bed. She did this to keep her feet warm. I lifted the cardigan and returned it to her bedside chair, and replaced it with a smallish blanket.

Thanks, she said without smiling, and added, Did ye go to the pub?

I told you I didnt.

You were a bit late home.

Yeh.

She continued watching me.

I shrugged. She was waiting. I just walked up and down, I said. I got off the bus and just eh, I walked up and down for a wee bit; coming to terms with things I suppose.

So you did get sacked.

I returned her look then glanced at the radio. No fancy a bit of music?

But she was not going to give up, gony gie up, she wasnay gony. People are strange. Wives especially; their tenacity makes them doubly so. I wonder if they are like that with other women, or is it just with men. It aint a question. I call it a noggin-shaker, as in 'one shakes one's noggin'.

Cath, I said, I need to say something: it was important what happened with that shit. I'm no taking crap off the likes of him. What, because he's my gaffer I'm supposed to shut my mouth! Never. It is not life or death, granted, but we still cannay allow it. I am not going to allow it. Right wing fucking bastard, I am telling ye, guys like him, Labour Party bastards, they put the Tories to shame, fascist cunts. That is who they put in charge, that is so-called Britain and the fucking ppolitical system.

Cath watched from the safety of the sheets and duvet.

But it is a serious thing, I said, we are talking here about working-class representation. Bloody joke.

197

Yes well write yer book, she said, ye've wasted enough time.

I shall write it.

Fine.

Some of us are not going stand for it any longer. I mean are we supposed to let them walk over the top of us? Fucking bunch of gangsters. You think I'm past it, well I'm no past it. If you think I am, I'm no.

No what, past what, did I miss something?

I dont actually care, I said, honestly, I dont. I'm forty-two years of age. Do ye know what we talk about during a typical tea-break in one's typical factory warehouse? How effing glad we shall be to reach one's seniority; in other words our chief desire is to become old-age pensioners. What happened to all our hopes and dreams! That is what happened to them. This is what I am talking about, give me the happy pills. Great Britain today, the existential nightmare that would have driven my poor old father off his fucking nut if he hadnay had the good sense to die at the advanced age of sixty-one and three quarters. So-called Scotland, be it known, a complete waste of space: I refer here to one's existence.

I wish I was a pensioner already. I want to go to a green field and just lie down. I want to get put out to graze like these old horses that win the Grand National, nay hustle and bustle. Just chewing the cud. Mind you, I said, pausing with one's hand on the bedroom door handle. I would like to get him. Preferably down the back of the storeroom, thoughts of shifting spanners and skulls, crunch de la crunch.

Cath was looking worried re sanity, her partner's.

You dont know whether to believe me or not, I said.

He certainly is getting to you.

Oh jees.

He is.

Yeh, I said, I wake up thinking about him, go to sleep thinking about him. Fucking ratbag! Ach well. Want a cup of tea?

Eh . . .

Hot water with lemon?

How did ye guess?

I smiled. I'm gony have toast, d'ye no want some? Take some toast. The little essentials in life, toast and marmalada madame, eh, you want, you want me I serve you brekadafast ladeee, my leetil dandeelion senorita.

Cath looked at me.

Ye sure? I said.

No thanks.

Sorry about this stupid male shite.

Mm.

I continued into the kitchen, filled the kettle, standing next to the sink. And the window. From here I looked straight upwards, over the tenement roofs facing. It was a flight path. I enjoyed seeing the planes, these long-haul destinations, desert islands and nice hotels. Month holidays. People needed month holidays in foreign domains. No bosses, no gaffers, no Scottishness or Britishness.

There was a sound behind. Her arms were round me while I was dumping the teabag into one's mug. I stopped what I was doing. She held me tightly. She was wearing only her nightdress. I cannot move, I said.

I'm not letting ye move.

You are so warm and cuddly.

Just relax.

I have to get the milk, I said.

Relax.

I did relax. After a moment I sighed. My shoulders drooped. Man, fuck, I felt it, man, for fuck sake man oh man gaffers and all sorts, out the fucking windi

amazing, how I felt, how it happened. I heard the water approach boiling point and freed my right arm, ready to pour it into the mugs. That is our rightful tradition, I said, to be felt by others as we feel them.

You just cannot relax, she said.

I can, I'm just eh preparing to pour the water.

She sighed, irritated. She was, and it was my fault. She walked to collect her cigarettes. They were next to the microwave. We had a wee hi-fi system beside it. Not fancy some music? Put something on, I said.

What?

Anything.

What like?

I scratched down beneath the lobe of my ear then my scalp, watching her light a cigarette. She had a range of nightdresses. They were all kind of silly, with bunny-rabbit patterns, teddy bears. With her figure they were a bit incongruous, thank christ, she didnay have what they call a girlish figure. She skipped through the CDs, barely reading their covers. The *Karelia*'s a cassette, I said.

Oh I'm not playing a cassette.

Well whatever, whatever ye like.

You always want Sibelius.

I dont always want Sibelius, I'll take Hazel Dickens.

If you want the cassette go and get it. I can never find anything in there, it's a complete mess.

I watched her inhale on the cigarette, a really long sort of deep inhalation as befits one who enjoys a smoke, like myself, who wrapped it all in a year ago and have regretted it ever since, unlike one's nearest and dearest who has a fancy card pinned on the wall which reads; This belongs to a Happy Smoker!

Hurreh! That is what I shout whenever I see it. Now she gied me a wifely look. Is that smoke good? I said.

She winked.

Blow it ower here will ye! I clutched at the smoke and inhaled loudly. Ye know something, I said, things havenay been the same in the factory since Jimmy Robertson retired.

Mm.

That's the truth.

Cath nodded.

I mean really, old Jimmy, christ. You never saw him but ye knew he was there. That last year, they put him out in the gatehouse.

That wasnt fair.

I nodded.

It wasnt.

Naw. Although he preferred it . . . he said he did anyway – fuck, that guy was a beacon. Ye aye knew: here is one guy that still exists in the world, a proper reader, a proper thinker, somebody that knows pppolitics and fucking fuck knows what, history! Everything!

Dont look for excuses.

Excuses for what?

To finish with yer job. If ye want to finish the job then finish it.

I am finished with it.

Cath smiled at me for a moment.

I am finished with it, I said.

Oh.

I didnt think you were listening to me.

I was.

I am finished with it.

She nodded.

At least with Jimmy I could talk about stuff. See that crowd nowadays, they are so ignorant. But they think they know everything. They actually believe the Scottish Nationalists are a left wing party, them and the Lib-Dems. Honest! But at the same time if ye want to vote socialist ye vote for the Labour Party. Unless ye're an extremist. In that case ye vote for the Scottish Socialists! Honest, that's what they think. Ye ever heard such crap! But they actually believe it.

Cath sighed.

They know nothing so they cannay think. They cannay think because they know nothing.

She might have been listening to me. She lifted an ashtray from the mantelpiece, planked herself down on the one armchair in the entire room, laying the ashtray beside her on the shoogly fucking wee coffee table that aye collapsed if I even looked at the stupid thing. She pulled her legs up, covering her shoulders with a woolly article, tugging the nightdress down to cover her legs. She inhaled on the cigarette and shivered. I was about to walk to her but my foot kicked a teddy bear. Imagine that, a teddy bear. My daughters were ten and twelve and they still fucked about with teddy bears.

I hated using the word 'fuck' when referring to one's offspring. But there we are.

Look at that, I said, and stooped to pick it up. It's got one of these ears ye see on the *Antiques Roadshow*.

No it's not.

It's probably worth an effing fortune!

If it's got a button in the ear. Only if.

Is that right?

Yeh.

Christ.

Cath smiled.

Why dont you go to night school and do a course on antiques. I think you could earn a fortune. You have a feel for it. At the same time . . .

Yes?

I shrugged.

Cath was looking at me.

Fancy a go?

What?

Nothing.

You're so edgy.

I'm not.

Then ye jump down my throat.

I dont really, it's just the way it comes out. Things get to me. I try not to let them but they do. Just now they do. It's no to do with being edgy, I just get a tight feeling.

Oh so you want me to worry about heart attacks?

Not at all. I raised my hand to my upper chest and rubbed in a circular motion.

She watched me. Have ye got indigestion?

A touch.

She swung her legs down from the seat. She said, I take it ye were talking about sex?

Who me?

I know you.

You know me!

I do.

Ye think ye know me.

Okay, she said, but were you talking about sex?

Yes but we'll have a drink of tea first.

She swung her legs back onto the seat. Called yer bluff as usual.

I chuckled, passing her a mug of hot water with a dod of lemon floating about.

Just relax, she said, for a change.

My feet will be freezing.

Good.

What d'ye mean good!

Cath smiled. Wash them, that will heat them up. They're probably ponging.

Oh man.

Some people would go for a shower.

But I'm just finished my work!

Dont wheedle.

Well really, I'm not wheedling. I paused, smiled in a conspiratorial manner. You think you've got the upper hand dont you?

She exhaled smoke towards me. I awaited her comment. None came. I closed my eyes. I thought she might have spoken then but she didnt. Thus I would have to.

No. I didnt have to, not at all. Of course I didnt, nobody is obliged to speak. Sometimes I cannay get the hang of that obvious truth, people like me, we cant. And evil fuckers like the gaffer play on it. Honest. Will we ever be free of the shite, the degradation — because that is what it is, degradation. We are degraded man! Will they ever leave us alone? Ye wonder but.

Cath gazed at me.

Ye know what he called me? A throwback; he called me a throwback.

What did you do?

Me?

Yes.

What did I do? I cannot remember.

Is he afraid of you?

You joking?

I wouldnt be too sure.

He's paranoiac right enough.

There ye are, said Cath.

He thinks I've got the young team on my side.

Who?

The younger ones. He thinks they listen to me. They do but only about football; only if I dont lecture them about ppppolitics; they cannay cope with ppppolitics.

Cath listened but was not smiling. I saw the anxiety. Smoke didnt relax her. I was glad I had stopped.

I wished I could help her stop. I wished I could help her period. Just about the future, I wasnay sure about the future. It was a long time till I retired. Maybe we could go someplace. Anyway, she was going back to work herself. If she could get a job. She spoke about getting a job but how did she know she would get one, she didnay even know she would get one, fucking dreamworld.

Oh man.

What is it? she said.

I spoke out loud eh . . .! I smiled. Come here, take a look outside the window. Come on! Take a look! Blue sky . . . nothing but blue sky.

She made no move. She held the mug of tea in her right hand, closeby her cheek. I like the way women do that; every last ounce of heat, ye want to extract it.

Intract it, she said.

Intract it! Take it out and put it in.

James Kelman

Dont be vulgar.

I smiled. Cath puffed on her cigarette. Or interact, I said. That must be where the word comes from.

Where's the toast? Did ye not make toast? I thought ye were hungry?

To be honest, no.

I'll make ye something.

Dont bother.

I'll just finish my smoke first.

I can make it myself.

Cath smiled. I watched her inhale again on the cigarette. Two puffs in two seconds. What if she died? I nodded. If you dont stop smoking you will die. Do ye know that?

She blew smoke at me. I grinned and shouted at the ceiling. Heh God! there's a woman down here trying to kill herself!

Cath covered her mouth with her right hand: Oh ya blaspheming pig ye, you'll go to Hell.

She was really laughing and I laughed too. I swallowed some tea, set the mug on the arm of the chair, then transferred it to the floor. She was watching me. I reached down and lifted it, transferred it to a safer place, the damn table.

Good boy.

I saluted her. Mon capitaine. I returned to the window. There are scarecrows down below skipper. Think I should toss them a lifeline? I cupped my hand to my mouth: Leave them to suffer bosun, leave them to suffer! It's the only way they'll learn. Aye aye sir!

What ye blethering about!

Nothing, I'm just cracking up.

Linda's coming home at dinner time.

What about dinner school?

She asked to stay off.

206

My God. In my day we would have gave wur eyeteeth for school dinners.

Cath was stubbing her cigarette out.

Far below the window the docile subjects wended their weary way back and forward and back and forward.

Is that you talking to yerself again!

I always think of that painting by Brueghel, the one with the all the people, and the horses and dogs; the village scene.

You're wrong to think of that one.

How come?

Because it is the slaughter of the innocents.

Christ, aye.

Your memory is not good.

I know, it is like a mental collapse has occurred. My synapses have collapsed. Death by collapsing synapses. For all I know it's a recognised industrial disease, brought on by constant nightshift.

We need to get away.

Mayo!

Not Ireland.

I'd love to go to Ireland.

Not me.

I wish we could.

We cant.

What about the Hebrides?

Oh god.

Sorry.

I just wish . . .

What?

Nothing.

I closed my eyes tightly. There are choices to make and we've got to make the right yin. We do, we have to! I slapped my forehead with my right hand, then again. And this time a real fucking sore yin and it made a loud slapping noise. Jesus christ, I said, that was sair!

Dont expire yet.

I gave an exaggerated groan, clutching at my chest: They're taking my life's blood, the last breath in me body.

Relax. Come to bed.

I'll no sleep.

Ye will.

I'll have to masturbate and I'm too old to masturbate. Honest, I blush when I do it.

Ye're just exhausted, yer last shift of the week.

My last shift period.

Oh so ye have been sacked!

I smiled. I opened the window wider, to let out the tobacco fug. Not to jump, I said, to let in some air. I feel kind of jittery, like I'm defenceless.

I scratched my mouth, wiped round it quite roughly. It is true, I am defenceless. The next time the gaffer looks at me the wrong way I'm liable to burst out greeting. That is the kind of man I am, the kind of guy you're married to.

I like the guy I'm married to.

Naw but nay kidding ye Cath— I stopped and stared out the window, straining to see further below, my head angling. My goodness look at that, I said.

What, what are you looking at?

God knows.

Is she attractive?

Not as attractive as you. I faced her now, folding my arms. You thought I was past it?

Past what?

Would ye leave me if I was?

You do get some juvenile ideas.

I shook my head, looked back out the window. Sometimes I just want to lie and stare up at the sky, see if I can spot some stars.

During the day?

Sure, why not? If ye want to look and see ye should be able to . . . I wiped spittle from the corner of my mouth. I could do with a smoke myself.

Well you're not getting one, she said.

I dont want one.

That's all we need, you starting again.

It's the smell, sometimes I . . .

Cath smiled. She left her cigarette smouldering in the ashtray and came towards me. I made space for her to see out the window, put my arm round her shoulder. Far below a woman was passing along the pavement and entering our very close. It made us both smile. I find that very positive, I said.

Cath chuckled.

Who is she? I said.

Missis Taylor, she lives one up.

Honestly?

Yeh.

God! I laughed.

She looked at me steadily, unsmiling. I kissed her on the forehead, cupped her chin in my hand, angling my head to kiss her on the lips. She was always so cool, so calm, but I could never have told her that, never.

And she wouldnt have believed me, she didnt believe me, it wasnt true, it was just shite, it was nonsense. I broke from her and she frowned, then smiled. What's up?

Nothing, I said.

LIZ LOCHHEAD

Born in Motherwell in 1947 and a Glasgow resident today, Liz Lochhead graduated from Glasgow School of Art in 1970, the decade during which she – alongside Alasdair Gray, Tom Leonard and James Kelman – became a member of Philip Hobsbaum's creative writing group.

Lochhead is one of Scotland's leading playwrights, with a considerable body of work including *Blood and Ice* (1982), the contemporary classic *Mary Queen of Scots Got Her Head Chopped Off* (1987), *Cuba* (1997), *Perfect Days* (1998) and *Good Things* (2006). Plays she has adapted and given a Scots voice to include Bram Stoker's *Dracula* (1989), Euripides's *Medea* – for which she won the 2001 Saltire Society Scottish Book of the Year Award, Sophocles's *The Theban Plays*, Chekhov's *Three Sisters*, the *York Mystery Cycle* and Molière's *Tartuffe* and *Le Misanthrope* (as *Misery Guts*).

Lochhead's prowess as poet, too, is in no doubt: in 1972 she won a Scottish Arts Council Book Award for her collection of poems, *Memo for Spring* and, taken together, two of her subsequent collections – *Dreaming Frankenstein* (1984) and *The Colour of Black and White* (2003) – encompass thirty years of her poetry since 1967. *Scotland on Sunday* wrote of *The Colour of Black and White*, 'The intelligence and sociability of Lochhead's poetry . . . is something one hopes we will always have in Scotland.'

NOT CHANGED

Liz Lochhead

You've not *changed*! Not changed? I mean what are folk like?

Don't start me.

What are they like? Well, obviously not everybody, not everybody. It takes all kinds, it does, you don't let it . . . Well, you do, you sometimes do, but you know you shouldn't. Feel paranoid in any way. You try to tell yourself there's been a lot on the TV about gender reassignment, because there has recently, and, och, when it comes down to it most folks attitude is it takes all kinds live and let live, no skin off my nose.

Nine times out of ten course they're *curious* but they're not actually bothered. One way or the other.

Course some are. So cruel. Really. They can be.

Michele Quigley. Michele bloody Quigley. I mean one minute I'm quite the thing swanning around Markses thinking I'll treat myself to a new forty-two B because they've got some really pretty stuff in since they've bounced back, even in the bigger sizes. Next thing I'm in the middle of Per Una in floods.

Because I coped at the time. Acquitted myself. You generally do but how I got myself down that escalator to ground God knows. Then straight out the door and across to that Newsbox for a packet of fags, first in vernear a year, and straight in here to the Shopper's Ladies and, do you know, I'd have lit up, I would of, if I didn't at the back of my mind believe in the guff about smoke alarms. Don't do it. Just don't.

Naw, I'm not going to.

What the hell Michele Quigley had to be doing on the till at the lingerie. As well it was empty!

Goes: Michael! Michael Manson! My god, I'd have known you anywhere. You've not changed.

Felt like saying couldn't say the same for you darling. Fifteen stone if she was an ounce. Twice the size. All that blubber and in there, underneath . . . the old Michele. I'd have known her anywhere anall.

Turns out she's been down here best part of twenty years. Came down with the ex when the weans were wee, not been back much, and nothing to take her now her mother and faither are both away. Goes: I've not lost the accent, but! You can take the girl out of Glasgow but you can't take the Glasgow out of the girl.

She says: what brung you to this neck of the woods?

Well, I felt like saying, what do you think?

I mean, it's not famous for tolerance, Scotland, is it? There are those that say it's changed, it's no different fae anywhere else and yes, many folk in my situation do relocate, it's understandable I suppose, but all I know is it never occurred to me, or to Maureen, that staying at home was any kind of an option. We're not big on new beginnings, are we? And Michele Quigley's attitude more or less proves I was right.

Bloody cigarettes. Gasping. But I shouldn't. I mustn't. I can't. I'm not going to. I'm no.

Michele goes: Oh Michael.

I says it's Michele, Michele.

She says No Michael *I'm* Michele.

I says: I'm Michele.

She goes *no I'm Spartacus* and starts laughing. She says: no I'm sorry it's just what is it with yous . . .? You know, how come you don't change your name totally, how come all the Johns become Jo-annes and the Matts Matilda and the Phils Phyllis? Why go to all that bother just for a little feminine appendage? How do you not go from like Boab Smith to . . . like . . . Lolita Angelica Lopez or something? How is it just goodbye Sam hello Samantha and the same old surname?

I says: I'm still the Same person.

She says *unless you called yourself after me?*

Sorry, I says, sorry. It's just . . . my old name. In a feminine form. Simple as that.

She says you're not though.

I says I'm not what?

She says: the same person.

And thing is that was where she was wrong. See, I could go out that door right now and look at myself in that mirror and know exactly who I see. Not everybody can do that. Can you? Total self acceptance. I told her that was the reason I had to go to all this length to change everything.

I said do you know what I really miss? The fags. Because conditional on me getting the op, obviously, is going one year fag-free. Surgeons insist on it. Anaesthetists. That and living and dressing as a woman full time.

She says: and passing?

I says well Michele I can't say I've never clocked the odd funny look in a too slow-moving queue in the ladies (and aren't they all, that has been a revelation) but, you know, short of me getting desperate, hiking up ma skirt to ma neck and pishing in the sink people basically tend to be pretty polite and just zip their lips.

Because I do realise I'll never be a pretty woman. I mean I look at someone like Michele and she's been both. She's been one of the young and very visible ones – a stoater – and now she's one of the invisible ones and she sees me stepping, voluntarily, onto the moving wheel at this stage of the game, the downer, post-menopausal (not that that exactly applies to me, but . . .) and she just doesn't get it. At all.

She said: You couldn't get enough of my tits.

I said: no Michele I couldn't.

She was gorgeous. And now oh my god the arse on her. How are the mighty fallen.

Bitter but. That's the bit I don't get. When my wife can, twenty-four year in, find it in her heart to uproot, relocate down here, live with me as my sister and, ach, come out Mother of the Bride outfit shopping with me last week for something for me to put on at our son's wedding – because I'm going up, we both are, Maureen and me, thegither, because it's *our son* and we're going, whether or not it puts the ball on the slates with certain elements in the family, and he *wants* us both to be there, does our Mark, well, they both do, him and the girl, and it's their Big Day, so it's up to them and there's got to be hope for the future in that, eh?

And yet Michele Quigley I went out with for about six weeks, six weeks max, in 1979 couldn't look at me? Couldn't give me her blessing by getting her mouth around my name.

Straight out. Straight out and bought this packet of fags, opened it, stuck one in my mouth.

Not going to smoke it but.

Who needs them?

JACKIE KAY

Poet and novelist, Jackie Kay was born in Edinburgh in 1961 to a Scottish mother and Nigerian father and adopted by a white Scottish couple who brought her up in Glasgow. This experience inspired her first poetry collection, *The Adoption Papers* (1991) which won a Scottish Arts Council Book Award, the Saltire Society Scottish Best First Book of the Year Award and a commendation by the Forward Poetry Prize judges. She has written several other collections including *Other Lovers* (1993), *Off Colour* (1998) and *Life Mask* (2005); her book of selected poems, *Darling*, appeared in 2007 and a verse drama, *The Lamplighter*, followed in 2008 with a collection for children, *Red Cherry Red*.

Of *The Lamplighter*, *Scotland on Sunday* said it 'vividly show-cased the beauty and resilience of Kay's poetry, its ability to refresh memory and return dignity'. Kay was made an MBE in 2006.

Also an accomplished prose writer, Kay has written two

collections of short stories – *Why Don't You Stop Talking* (2002) and *Wish I Was Here* (2006); the latter won the British Book Awards Decibel Writer of the Year while her first novel, *Trumpet* (1998) won the *Guardian* Fiction Prize.

A series of Kay's monologues about Maw Broon is set for a Glasgow performance in October 2009 – the iconic Scottish matriarch who came to fame originally in the *Sunday Post*'s comic strip *The Broons*.

MIND AWAY

Jackie Kay

'There was something I wanted to remember, but I've forgotten now,' my mother was saying to me. 'The brain's a sieve. Maybe not a sieve, maybe a colander, the size of the things I'm losing,' my mother laughed. 'What was it? It's gone. If I don't say the minute something comes into my head, it goes. It's not so much that my thoughts are running away with me, more like they've run off with somebody else!'

'Who would that be?' I asked her.

'Oh, I don't know. Who would have them?'

'Who would you like to have them?'

'A young, dishy Doctor,' my mother said, without a moment's hesitation.

'We'll need to do a bit of private investigating and see if we can track him down,' I said. I suddenly had an idea, and things seemed doable. I poured myself a small malt to go with my idea. I nosed it first – three, four, five times, swirling the whisky in the glass around and around, and sniffing deeply: a childhood smell from the pine woods, a wood-smoke fire outside, a black stick of liquorice. I sniffed again, what else? I think I could smell the smell I used to smell on holidays in Yell, a smell of peat bog. I remember my mother and me in the Windy Dog café eating soup, not long before she lost her marbles.

'Here you!' she said, 'It's the middle of the afternoon. Is it not a bit early for the whisky?' Strange how some things still didn't get past her.

'I'm forty-four,' I said. 'It's cold outside, nothing like a wee nip to warm you up. Besides, all private investigators keep a bottle of Scotch in their seedy offices!'

My mother's eyes shone with delight. 'This is the best idea you've had in a long time!' she beamed.

'I'm certain he'll be a NHS man. He'll not be a BUPA Doctor! Not in a million years! Come on Nora Gourdie,' she said to herself, trying to put her tights on, rolling them over her fist and aiming her flesh foot into the foot of her opaque tights with reinforced toes. I got out my old Olivetti and typed away; it was the only thing that stopped my migraine, paradoxically, the sound of typing.

Doctor Mahmud was sitting in his surgery with his patient Peter Henderson when Doctor Mahmud suddenly said, 'I'm finding I don't like wearing tights anymore. It's a hassle pulling them up and over my ankles, my knees. I'm that exhausted when I've hoisted them over my knickers that I've lost the will to live. Time *Sheer* and I parted company!'

'Pardon?' Peter said. Doctor Mahmud had just finished writing a prescription in his rather erratic and mostly illegible handwriting. Peter Henderson was fifty-six, and had just been told his cholesterol was sky-high and he would need to start taking cholesterol pills and cut down on certain foods. Peter was feeling morose, and a little jumpy. 'Sorry?' Peter said. 'What were you saying?' But the Doctor just stared at him blankly as if he hadn't said a thing. Just being in the Doctor's surgery reminded Peter that he was going to die. Alright, not for a while yet, but it was going to happen. It wasn't kidding on, death. It would come for him, like it had come for his mother, his wife, his old pal Duncan.

Doctor Mahmud was a handsome big bugger, slim, fit, sympathetic, usually. Peter Henderson was huge, hefty; he barely fitted into the Patient's seat. Peter perched on the end of it and waited for the Doctor to speak. He sat with his legs splayed open because they were too fat to close. He'd been brought up to revere a Doctor's thoughts. The thing about this cholesterol was that you couldn't eat any of your favourite things anymore, which made you wonder not if life was worth living exactly, but if life was rich enough to live, if it had enough flavour. What was the point in going through the motions of life without deep-fried Mars Bars, bloody steaks, streaky bacon and eggs, a poke of chips and curry sauce? The future was oily fish, spinach, rocket, watercress, Christ!

'It's all about unsaturated fat,' Doctor Mahmud said.

'I'll Google fat when I get home the night,' Peter said, in a thin voice.

'No. Google makes people paranoid. Too much information! Stay away from Google!'

'Right,' Peter laughed a little nervously. What was it with the Doctor the day? Was he just going off on one?

'There's really nothing to worry about,' the Doctor said, frowning. 'We'll do another blood test in six weeks to measure your levels again.'

'Thank you, Doctor. Will the pills have any side effects?' Peter asked, staring at the weighing scales in the Surgery, and feeling a moment's relief that he hadn't been asked to stand on them.

'No, you won't notice anything. There are people with worse problems. Cholesterol? Many people have high cholesterol. Eh? We're living in the age of cholesterol. This is not the age of Aquarius!'

Peter laughed, not his usual big booming laugh, but a little squeaky, quirky *eee hee hee*. His beer belly hung over his trousers like a ridge over a mountain. Little beads of sweat assembled on his forehead for a chat. He was just about to lumber himself out of the Patient's seat when the good Doctor suddenly shouted:

'The snags, the rips, the ladders! Why did any of us bother? Why didn't we wear trousers years ago?'

'Excuse me?' Peter said again to the Doctor, thinking perhaps there was also something going wrong with his hearing. These days when Peter watched the television, particularly soaps, he heard a small voice underneath the actors' whispering stage instructions. *Maria closes the door and walks to Underworld, the knicker factory.* The Doctor's white coat, his stethoscope, his blood pressure pump, his neat desk, all of that was the same as usual, but what was happening to the Doctor's conversation? Peter looked at the people waiting to see a Doctor. Little do you know what you're in for, he thought, looking at the anxious young Mum with her snotty-nosed baby. He popped his head through the reception hatch.

'Doctor Mahmud says another appointment in six weeks?' the receptionist said.

Peter nodded and sighed. A single tear trickled down his ruddy cheek. He picked up his prescription and exited the surgery so fast he was sure that he could feel his cholesterol level hitting the sky.

Alone in his surgery, Doctor Mahmud washed his hands with surgical cleaner at the small, low sink in the corner. He dried his hands on a paper towel and looked in the mirror. His hair was neat enough; his small beard was well-trimmed, his eyes were a little dark underneath. He was trying to think when it first started. There was nothing in any of his symptoms that he recognised. He was thirty-three years old, and was enjoying being part of the Springfield Practice. He worked alongside two brilliant Doctors. (Though Mahmud would have to admit – if pushed – that he was the most popular of the three; patients clamoured to see him.) If it happened again, he'd have to go and see somebody.

'Do you think,' my mother was saying to me, 'that if I found the right Doctor, I'd get my train of thoughts back?'

'Absolutely!' I said.

'You gotta hope!' my mother said. 'Without hope, we're all done for. Pass the *Yellow Pages*.'

I'd stopped typing; the migraine was on its way out, hopefully, though I still felt a little queasy; perhaps the whisky would settle my stomach. I flicked through a lifestyle column in last Sunday's paper. It was an article on how well Meryl Streep has aged and how many different parts she's played.

'You'd never think Meryl Streep was just ten years younger than you,' I muttered, though my mother's face wasn't very lined.

'Botox! Is she on the Botox? Or is it the liposuction? What's the difference again? Does one put things in and the other suck things out? That's what's happening to me. My mind's lip-sucked! Yep. My mind's lip-sucked,' she repeated.

'That sounds rude!' I said.

'Even that Sudoku's no going to help me now,' she said. 'Oh Sudoku, Sudoku, what do you know, about a woman like me?' My mother was half singing, searching the *Yellow Pages* for health centres. I knew I was in for a period of darkness. I poured another measure of my Islay's cask 33.70, only sniffing twice this time. Ye canny go sniffing your life away. There was a sweet note somewhere, maybe a little too sweet – honey? Maple syrup?

'It takes ages to remember what letters come where these days! When you were younger, the alphabet was a skoosh, mental arithmetic was a doddle. I blame the government,' my mother exclaimed.

'You've lost me,' I said. I was trying to guess her meaning – Brown bailing out the banks? Student fees? Teaching standards?

'Everyone's so childish these days! No one can do a bloody thing! They've made infants of the lot of us! You can't get into your car without the bloody beeps coming on if you've not fastened your seat belt. What if you don't want to fasten your silly seatbelt?' she shouted. 'What if you'd prefer to take your chances?'

'Time for Mozart!' I said to my mother. I'd read somewhere that listening to Mozart slowed down Alzheimer's. At least I think I'd read that; I couldn't be sure. I was forgetting things myself. I put on Mozart's trio for clarinet, viola and piano in E Flat, K 498. It consoled me that Mozart was said to have composed this during a game of skittles. My mother sat and listened with her eyes closed, the *Yellow Pages* on her lap. A little tear rolled down her face. Music moved her and music helped my migraine. I imagined my mother dancing, years ago, dancing in an elegant polka dot dress. I pressed pause when the piece was finished. Our lives had turned around: I used to love *Watch with Mother;* now I loved Listen with Mother.

Music seemed to work every time. She always remembered what she'd just been doing.

'Bishopbriggs,' my mother said, pointing her finger at *Springfield Health Clinic.* 'Why don't we try the good Doctors of Bishopbriggs? (Doesn't that sound like the title to something? *The Good Doctors of Bishopbriggs.)* Years ago I remember going for dinner in a place called Stakis in Bishopbriggs with my pal Nancy Henshaw. I had a gammon steak with pineapple and Nancy had scampi and chips. We were over-the-moon. We thought we were the peak of sophistication!' My mother was laughing at the memory of herself when her hair was darker and her teeth her own and her mind, her mind agile, quick as a young hare running over a field of bluebells.

'You remember years ago with uncanny detail,' I complimented her.

'*Years ago* is not the problem. Yesterday is the problem. Today is the problem. Who do you think put gammon steak and pineapple together? I'll tell you one thing it wouldn't have been the prime minister,' my mother said.

'Maybe it was the opposition,' I said entering into the spirit of things.

'I get you!' my mother said, nudging me fiercely with her right elbow. 'Eh?' she said elbowing again.

'Opposites attract!' I said, smiling.

'Well your father and I were definitely opposites,' she laughed. 'I was good looking and he wasn't.' The tears poured again. 'Have you found him yet? This handsome Doctor?'

'Well we can't tell if they are handsome from their names unfortunately,' I said. I smiled, a silly little smile; I could feel it on my face. I could feel the good heat from the whisky in my stomach. My stomach was nice and empty so that I'd get the full hit of it. There was a kind of a roar as it went down, like my body was a furnace and I was throwing the flame down.

'Well, let's take pot luck then. Someone's got to know something,' my mother said darkly. 'You can't just have words disappearing in the dead of night and nobody bothering their shirt! Someone's bound to have noticed something! Somewhere!'

'Ha!' I said, 'Absolutely!' I was thinking what lovely company this Alzheimer's was for my drunken paranoia.

My mother was reading names out: Dr B. Gordon, Doctor C. Berg, Dr I. T. McNicholl, Dr Robert Mair, Doctor P. MacBrayne, Dr M. Mahmud. 'How about we try all of them?' I said.

'How will I know which one to pick?' My mother said anxiously.

'It's not you doing the picking! He's already chosen *you*, this Doctor whoever he is! He's already *got* your thoughts!'

'Oh my god,' my mother said, gripping my arm. 'You're not wrong. What a moment of lucidity! Right let's get out there and find him. What have we got to lose? Isn't life an awfully big adventure? Who was it who said that again? I've forgotten.'

I took the sheet out of the Olivetti. It hadn't quite worked the way I'd planned. The only thing that was consistent was the way the letter h was missing, it tried to hit h, but then only left a ghost of an h there. The trut was I was terrified, terrified of losing my mot er, not of er dying but of losing er because s e was losing erself is ow t at sentence would look if I typed it out. It was ard to keep track of w at I was saying wit t e missing.

These days we were spending so much time standing in the street – my mother trying to remember where it was she wanted to go. Once she was determined we went to her church for a bowl of soup in the church café. I had never been to her church and had no idea where it was. I was a non-believer anyway. She'd changed her faith when I was a teenager. We stopped and asked a policeman for directions; he leaned out of the window of his police car and looked into my mother's eyes. If only we could go to Lost Property and claim her mind back I thought; if only it'd been left at Left Luggage. The policeman didn't know; there were three churches nearby, and my mother couldn't remember the name. So we went into her hairdresser's at the corner of our street, and asked them. 'Excuse me?' my mother said. 'Where is my church?' The hairdresser shook her glossy hair and looked a little nonplussed. We left.

'It's like our own little pilgrimage,' I said to my mother, consolingly. She was getting very agitated.

'Oh your father would be angry with me by now.'

'Don't be silly, it's an adventure, our awfully big adventure,' I said.

'Who said that again? Did somebody just say that?' she said.

I put my arm through hers and we walked along the street adjacent to her house. The trees were losing their leaves, the birds were losing their feathers, the pound was losing its value and my mother was losing her mind. It was cold, freezing cold. 'We're in for a cold snap,' my mother said. 'I think it might snow later.'

Eventually we found it, and we had our bowl of soup and Nora beamed with pleasure. 'Nora enjoys a good bowl of soup,' my mother said to me. She loved characterising herself in this way, as if she was somebody else – perhaps she was now. The soup was religiously good – barley, carrots, and potatoes, and chicken. 'What's the name of these wee soft bits? What was I going to tell you?' My mother said and shook her head, looking a little stunned, surprised at herself, as if on the edge of something uproarious.

Doctor Mahmud said to the young mother with the baby on her lap, 'There's nothing like a good bowl of soup. It warms up the old heart. Mind, you've got to cut the pieces wee enough. You dinny want to choke on your soup!' Then he got up abruptly and washed his hands. The back of his hands were very hairy. More hairy than usual? He wasn't sure. It was no joke now.

'I think she's too young for solids,' the young mother said. Her baby was ten days old. Doctor Mahmud ran his fingers through his hair. He would have to take some time off. He couldn't go on like this. So far there'd been no complaints; but it was only a matter of time. The Doctor would have to get to the root of it. You couldn't practice as a reputable GP shouting at people in this manner! It was appalling. It was against everything he'd been taught. He turned back around and put his thermometer under the baby's arm. The baby was crying, a high-pitched newborn's cry.

'Barley! That's the name! Barley!' he shouted in his broad old woman's voice over the din of the greeting bairn. The baby stopped crying instantly. Out of the blue, there was a lovely spacey silence in the surgery between the baby, the Doctor and the mother. The Doctor looked out of his window. Snowflakes drifted dreamily and the Doctor said pleasantly, 'Plenty fluids, no cause for alarm. You're breastfeeding?'

The mother nodded. Everything about being a new mum was terrifying. The world was suddenly a terrifying place. She found herself bursting into tears when she watched the news. What had she done bringing a baby into a world like this? 'Doctor,' she said, tentatively, 'I'm feeling worried about the world.'

'This is normal. All new mums want world peace!'

'I'm worried she'll grow up in a world where she'll never see a Panda,' she cried. The tears rolled down her cheeks.

'Don't worry.' For the first time that day, the Doctor could feel the other voice coming on. He had to get her out of the room before it spoke again. Maybe this was a good sign. Maybe it meant he could exercise some control. He ushered the young mum out and stood by his sink. It was strange. It felt as if it was getting closer, and the instances were becoming more acute. He had a sense of what it must be like being in labour – the panic of the contractions coming quicker and quicker.

My mother and I got off the train at Bishopbriggs. From Glasgow Queen Street to Bishopbriggs Cross was just seven minutes. We crossed over the railway bridge and walked down the slope at the other side.

'Where's Stakis? Can we find Stakis and have a gammon steak and pineapple?' my mother said.

'After the Doctor!' I said firmly.

'Oh yes, the Doctor. I forgot. I can picture him,' my mother said. 'He's handsome. He's Pakistani. He's got a small beard. He's tall. He's kind. He's got beautiful eyes. And a lovely set of teeth! His smile would melt an old woman's heart.'

'Goodness! I hope he exists!' I said wryly. I was starting to feel panicky. How would I get any new Doctor to see my mother? How would I explain her thinking about her lost thoughts? It was crazy. I should never have indulged her. I'd gone too far.

'He exists all right,' my mother said walking quickly up the road. There was nothing wrong with her mobility. She was faster than me. I was finding walking in a straight line a bit of a challenge. If my mother got her lost thoughts back, I'd give up whisky! That felt like a decent bargain. Three cars were waiting at the traffic lights under the old railway bridge. The lights changed.

'When we get there, you let me do the talking,' I said to my mother.

She nodded. 'I'm having the time of my life,' she said. 'We're cannier than Cagney and Lacey; we've got more irony than Ironside, we've got more hair than Kojak, nicer raincoats than Columbo, better sweaters than Starsky and Hutch, but we're not more stylish than, what's her name? Oh damn, it's gone. What's her name; you know the one, the one that had the wee drunken dance with her whisky?'

*   *   *

'Helen Mirren,' Doctor Mahmud said aloud to the mirror in his surgery. He called reception. 'No more patients for me today, please. I'm not feeling myself. Can you get Doctor Gordon and Doctor Berg to relieve me?' The receptionist sounded frazzled. 'What a figure for her age! Prime! Didn't they call her that for short! Prime!' Doctor Mahmud shouted down the receiver then hung up.

The receptionist pulled a face. Weirder and weirder! Outside the surgery, snow had started to fall in earnest.

Nora Gourdie stuck her tongue out. Snowflakes melted on her tongue. She pulled her red scarf around her neck. 'Do you think it's going to lie?' she asked her daughter. 'I hope it does. It's lovely when the snow covers everything, pretty, eh?'

'We are here,' I said. The snow was whirling now, dancing. I was feeling like a complete idiot, bringing my old mother out in the freezing cold in a flurry of flakes in search of a Pakistani Doctor. It was insane. It was another sign for me, that I was knocking it back too much. I'd lost all sense of judgement and propriety. 'You sit there,' I told her. 'I'll go and see what's what. You're going to come as a bit of a shock to him if he is here.' My mother nodded. Her eyes were shining.

'What if I fall in love with him?' she said. 'Oh, the snow's so romantic!'

'Excuse me,' I said at the reception. 'I wonder if you can help me? My mother's got what we think might be early onset Alzheimer's or dementia. We're not sure. And I wondered if she could see a Doctor here? We're visiting Bishopbriggs, you see, staying with friends. We've come down from Ullapool,' I lied.

'I'm sorry,' the receptionist said. 'We're inundated the day.'

'That's him! Look there he is!' my mother shouted springing to her feet and pointing excitedly at a tall handsome man leaving a room with a pile of files in his arms.

'Is he a Doctor?' I asked the receptionist.

'Yes, that's Doctor Mahmud, but he's not feeling well. He's going home early.'

'Do you know me? Do you know me like I know you?' my mother was saying. Doctor Mahmud stared at the small woman with grey hair in a red coat. There was something familiar about her. She wasn't one of his patients, he was certain of that. It wasn't her face that was familiar. What was it? He stood staring at her puzzled.

'He's the one! He's the one!' my mother shouted.

'I'm so sorry about this,' I said, approaching the Doctor. 'Is there any chance we could talk to you, privately, just for a few moments?'

'It'll take more than a few moments to get my thoughts back!' my mother said.

'Ssssssh,' I said. 'You'll just sound like a crazy woman to the nice Doctor here.'

It was her voice, Mahmud thought. Where had he heard that voice before? The Doctor approached the reception. 'I'm going to take this lady through to my surgery. She seems very distressed.'

'I thought you were going home, Doctor?' the receptionist said.

The snow was still falling, it probably would lie on top of walls on the way home; there'd be thick snow icing on the roofs of cars, white branches on trees, sparkling roofs, snowy, crunchy secret fields. It was beautiful, the soft, soft snow. The snowflakes were musical notes falling; Mahmud could hear Mozart's piano.

'No. I'm not going home right now. I'm feeling better,' Mahmud said, and smiled enigmatically. 'Through this way, please,' he took my mother's arm. She was in her element.

'I think I chose . . . What's the word, when you're careful?' she asked Doctor Mahmud.

'Responsible,' he said, because he already knew her thoughts and felt an extraordinary sensation of wonder and calm.

'You chose responsibly.'

'Exactly!' my mother said. Nora was beaming. She was as happy as snowflakes. Her face was flushed; she suddenly looked young again.

ROBIN ROBERTSON

Author of three collections of poetry, Robin Robertson has twice won the Forward Poetry Prize – first, in 1997 for his debut volume, *A Painted Field* (best first collection), and again in 2006 for his third, *Swithering* (best poetry collection). His second collection, *Slow Air*, was published in 2002. He received the E. M. Forster Award from the American Academy of Arts and Letters in 2004. He has also edited, among other works, *Mortification: Writers' Stories of their Public Shame* (2003) and is author of a critically acclaimed verse translation of Euripides' *Medea* (2008). His fourth collection will be published in early 2010.

Born in 1955 in Perthshire, Robertson was brought up on Scotland's north-east coast and now lives in London. In his role as deputy publisher at Jonathan Cape he has honed a fine stable of prize-winning authors and has been described as no less than 'formidable'.

Robin Robertson

A *Scotland on Sunday* profile of the poet said, 'His writing is clearly striving towards something which is much more rare – an almost painful emotional honesty. He believes curiosity is a powerful engine within poetry and that when life is at its most difficult, a writer should be most spiritually alert.'

THROUGH THE TWEED

Robin Robertson

Giving a back-rub
to Hugh MacDiarmid
I felt, through the tweed,
so much tension
in that determined
neck, those little
bony shoulders
that, when it was released,
he simply
stood up and fell over.

WILLIAM MCILVANNEY

Born in Kilmarnock in 1936, son of a former miner and brother of the sports journalist, Hugh, William McIlvanney won the 1975 Whitbread Prize for Fiction with his third novel, *Docherty* – McIlvanney's father took part in the General Strike of 1926 and the legacy of this experience informs *Docherty* and other books by the author.

His sequence of hard-hitting detective novels set in Glasgow – *Laidlaw* (1977), *The Papers of Tony Veitch* (1983) and *Strange Loyalties* (1991) – is said to have spawned the tradition of morally complex crime writing known as 'tartan noir', though the 'term does not appeal' to McIlvanney. His other novels include *The Big Man* (1985) – which was made into a feature film – *The Kiln* (1996) and most recently *Weekend* (2006).

As a poet, McIlvanney has three published collections to his name including *The Longships in Harbour* (1970), and he has written numerous volumes of essays and non-fiction derived from a prolific, high-profile career as a columnist and journalist.

He has won, among others, the Geoffrey Faber Memorial Award, the Saltire Society Scottish Book of the Year Award, two Crime Writers' Association Macallan Silver Daggers and, for his short story *Dreaming* – filmed by BBC Scotland in 1990 – a BAFTA.

Scotland on Sunday said, 'McIlvanney is a moralist as well as an artist . . . whose work is the fine fruit of a long engagement with what it means to be human and the question of how best we live our lives, of how we justify, obscurely and uncertainly, our existence.'

BURDALANE

William McIlvanney

Ablow the level o aa soond
Ayont aa space, behin
The fykemaleeries that abound
The daurk hertlands begin.

There ye will bide langer than time
To see anither gan –
Too faur tae cross, too heich tae climb.
The population's wan.

I dicht the brod wi careful cloot
An pit the buird-claith nait,
Try no to think that I'm aboot
Tae set a lanely plate.

William McIlvanney

I wash the flair though nae fit's traiked
Across it for sae lang,
Tryin no tae wish that there wis caked
Glaur o an orra thrang.

I scuff the stoor fae ma bit things
But dinna make them sheen
In case the whid o fushion brings
The sicht o me alane

The keekin-gless I aye wipe blin
Tae jouk the killin thocht
There in its blinter I micht fin
Masel: eydent for nocht.

The young yin in the deli said,
'It's for a pairty, ken,'
His bags stuffed fou o lang French breid,
Cauld meats, a kebbuck, wine.

His hair wis thick an glowin broon,
His een as bleck as taur.
He had a smile could licht a toon
A laugh tae stoap a war.

In him I saw much love tae be
An mony a smitten wumman
An weeshed me wan. He turned tae me
An winked an said, 'Ye comin?'

Ootsid the shoap there wis nae sign.
Bydin the bus wis sair.
Whaur he wis made ma auld hert dwyne
Nae buses rin tae there.

I had a veesitor the nicht
Afore the switch's wark,
Jist as the trimmle o the licht
Is swallied in the dark.

She cam as saft as waftin silk
She cam an didna talk.
Her flesh wis white as skyrest milk
An geck wis in her walk.

She skimmered in the gloamin room
An her bricht een were wild.
She lukked et me as I wis coom
An she wid not be fyled.

Disbelief wis aa she brung,
Wanhope wis aa she seen.
She wis masel when I wis young.
I wid she hadna been.

I didna ken whan we ganged that gate
The pleisure that waited in forlay.
I kent the guid days were steyin late
An shin they maun hervest the baurley,
An drubblie days no faur ahead
An winter wid tax me sairly.

But then the licht wis a warld o its ain
An Andra wis walkin aside me,
His haun a cantraip in mine agin pain
An his body a place I could hide me.
An the gleesh that ma hert et his touch had taen
Wis a bouet that ayewis wid guide me.

An sae, though that licht is lang awa
An withert the gress o oor beddin
An mony days noo are as bleck as a craw
An the morra is naethin I'm needin,
Inside it's still bricht as a wattergaw —
The day I had ludgins in Eden.

I took a lang, slow douk the nicht
Tae wash the absences awa
O Harry's een by candlelicht
An Tammas in the snaw,

O Andra in the simmer sun
When the licht turnt him tae gowd
There et the door as he cam in
An lust atween us lowed.

But pores themsels hae mind o things
An I cannae wash awa
Tint ends whaur rand crackin rings,
The tryst agin the wa.

An I gawked in the keekin-gless
An saw whaur cabbrach stauns,
Still in the runkles o the flesh
I kent their girnin hauns.

Sae here, as lanely wi me sits
In yae skin o cranreuch caul,
A wee gleid in the hert commits
Houghmagandie o the saul.

In the street I dinna see a street
I hear a watter roar,
See danger tae ilk soomin wean
A faur wey fae the shore.

There's naethin I can dae but tent
Their crouseness o their doom,
Fling oot daft thochts like lifebelts
An loue them as they soom.

The cauld's set up hame in ma banes the nicht,
Axin hoo lang I micht last,
An I'm hunkert roon the mind's wee licht
Tae warm ma auld hert et the past.

And there's no much ahead but trauchle an pine
An a single-en in the sod.
But I've had ma days when the warld wis mine
An I'm thinkin I micht forgie God,

William McIlvanney

Sae daith is the fled i the life
An we are the mice i the corn?
An this gled can see wi its peregrine e'e
An eemock that walks oan a thorn?
An ayewis the soond o the yeuck
Sweeshin nearer and nearer arron us?
And the dreid that we micht be kythed tae the licht
An the swouf o the gled up abune us?

Sae whaur can the gumpton be here?
Tae mak jeopardie hame an oan wuddrum be fed?
Weel, the corn is guid stuff, gin we gansh enough,
We micht stick in the craw o the gled.

A yet will open sometime shin.
There will be naebody there.
There micht be wrack across a muin,
A tree-lined loan, a square
That's glennie-lit, the oorie soond
O freens whas ettlin came
Tae gether oan auld weel-kent grund
An dinna mind yer name.
There will be laughin, no fae you.
Maisic that you micht hear
But never jig tae an a few
Wha luk, don't see ye there.

Hert will unfeeling then,
Mind ken it will never ken,
Whit ye wid dae, ye'll never dae
Again will never be again,
Trevel be steyin. Gae.

An afterword
by
William McIlvanney

Much of what passes for the Scots tongue today is a kind of residual
demotic gruel, a poorhouse version of the language. Given the
extent of the globalisation of culture in our time, this condition
is probably irreversible. Languages can wither. It happens. Who
knows what the Etruscans were trying to say?

What I hope will survive in a future Scotland is the style of
thought, the implicit philosophy the language gave us. Being like
English in its underwear, it always undercut pretentiousness. If
you have a geggie for a mouth and a bahookie for a posterior, that
tends to bring you down to earth a bit. Perhaps because it emerged
in response to a hard northern climate, Scots combined an ability
to confront the darkness of life with a talent for extracting a kind
of wry enjoyment from it. Substanceless optimism, which is how
the fashion seems to dictate we should be wearing our lives these
days, was never its forte.

In *Burdalane* (which means the last surviving member of a
family) an old woman reflects on her life in a language which is

William McIlvanney

largely dying with her. In her balancing act with the dark and the light I was trying to locate a kind of DNA of Scottish experience, something which would remind us of the source of who we are. I think we may need reminding. If you lose where you come from, you lose where you're going.

ANNE FRATER

Poet Anne Frater was born in 1967 on the Isle of Lewis and grew up speaking Gaelic as her first language. Her work has been published in her own collection *Fo'n t-Slige* (Under the Shell) in 1995 and in the anthologies *An Aghaidh na Sìorraidheachd* (1991), *An Anthology of Scottish Women's Poetry* (1991), *Siud an t-Eilean* (1993), *Dream State*: *The New Scottish Poets* (1994) and *An Tuil* (1999). She is also one of the contributors featured in *A History of Scottish Women's Writing* and *The Biographical Dictionary of Scottish Women* (published by Edinburgh University Press in 1997 and 2006 respectively) and in *An Leabhar Mòr* (Canongate, 2002).

Frater attended the University of Glasgow, from which she was awarded a PhD for her thesis, *Scottish Gaelic Women's Poetry up to 1750*, then worked as a media researcher and scriptwriter before returning to live in her native village, Pabail Uarach (Upper

Bayble) on Lewis. She is now a lecturer at the island's Lews Castle College, part of the UHI Millennium Institute, Gaelic degree courses.

AN STOIRM

Dha Murdina, Archie, Andrew agus Hannah

Anne Frater

Bha a' ghrian a-muigh
agus an latha cho ciùin;
oiteag bheag a' gluasad nan craobh
mar gum biodh nàire air a' ghaoth
i fhèin a nochdadh.

An dèidh mar a rinn i.

Trì làithean de shireadh
gus am faodamaid tòiseachadh
air ar caoidh;
an aon dòchas a bh' air fhàgail againn
gum bitheadh sibh còmhla anns an uaigh
mar a bha sibh còmhla anns a' bheatha
agus anns a' bhàs.

Anne Frater

A' ghrian gu h-àrd:
buidhe fann ann an adhar gorm
a' feuchainn ri ruaig a' chuir air na h-uisgeachan,
a' feuchainn ri fuachd a bhlàthachadh
a' feuchainn ris an dorchadas a shoillseachadh.

Gun fheum.

Na facail nach deach a ràdh
a' tuiteam nan deòir;
an inntinn nach gabhadh ris
a' sgreuchail gu sàmhach,
na gàirdeanan a bha gar h-iarraidh
a' greimeachadh càch a chèile:
an cràdh a' sìneadh a-mach a fhreumhan
gu gach duine aig an robh gràdh dhuibh.

Thuig sinn an latha sin na bha a' cunntadh:
chaidh sìtheanan na machrach a dhìth oirnn
's chan fhaicear am blàth tuilleadh.

THE STORM
For Murdina, Archie, Andrew and Hannah

The sun was out
and the day so calm;
a little breeze moving the trees
as if the wind were ashamed
to show her face.

After what she had done.

Three days of searching
before we could begin
to mourn;
the one hope remaining
that you would be together in the grave
as you had been in life
and in death.

The sun high above:
pale yellow in a blue sky
trying to disperse the waters,
trying to warm the cold
trying to light the darkness.

In vain.

The words that were unsaid
falling as tears;
the mind that could not grasp it
silently screaming,
the arms that reached for you
holding on to each other:
pain spreading out its roots
to everyone who loved you.

We understood that day what was important:
we had lost the machair flowers
and they will not bloom again.

A. L. KENNEDY

The Dundee-born (in 1965) writer and stand-up comedian, A. L. Kennedy has been listed twice (1993 and 2003) among *Granta*'s Best Young British Novelists. She is the author of five collections of short stories – *Night Geometry and the Garscadden Trains* (1990), *Now That You're Back* (1994), *Original Bliss* (1997), *Indelible Acts* (2002) and *What Becomes* (2009). Her five novels to date are: *Looking for the Possible Dance* (1993), *So I Am Glad* (1995), *Everything You Need* (1999), *Paradise* (2004) and *Day* (2007), which won the 2008 Costa Book of the Year Prize. In addition, among the many awards for her work she has won the John Llewellyn Rhys Prize, the Lannan Literary Award (fiction), the Austrian State Prize for Literature, the Saltire Society Scottish Book of the Year Award and Saltire Society Scottish Best First Book Award – and, while writer in residence for Hamilton and East Kilbride social work department, was awarded the Social Work Today Prize.

Kennedy also writes non-fiction – *On Bullfighting* (1999) and

A. L. Kennedy

The Life and Death of Colonel Blimp (1997) – and has written extensively for television (with John Burnside), the stage and radio. In the words of *Scotland on Sunday* she is 'a singular, superlative author'.

BLACKTHORN WINTER

A. L. Kennedy

His earliest adult experience – he wakes up in a hospital wearing someone else's clothes. Also there is a difference in his head. He is not alarmed, the boy, only puzzles in the cloth- and sour-tasting darkness of the ward until he knows it *is* a ward and that something has gone wrong and put him here.

'Nurse?'

The boy does not say this. He would never have thought to call a nurse: his character is undemanding and, besides, he cannot imagine needing anything beyond perhaps an explanation for the maritime rush which is catching at his ears and this dizzy, laden, weakness of his thinking.

'Nurse?'

It is this word that woke him, he believes – its repetition. First word of his alternate life.

'Nurse?'

Footfalls consent to be summoned and close, as fast as irritation

257

– heelthumps before toethumps and a squeak each time they argue with the floor.

The nurse's shape halts three beds down from the boy and interrupts the glimmers of a window in a way which seems peculiarly shocking.

'What do you want, then?'

She is nothing like the boy's mother, has a voice which is entirely strange to him, and sharpened – it sews through the air, passes over him, then on. He hears it ting against the farthest wall.

'Well ?'

'Can I have a glass of water?' The melody of the question is indecisive, apologetic.

'No.'

And the nurseshape begins to leave again, even more quickly, while the boy wonders if the other child, the thirsty one – who sounds like a boy, too – will maybe die soon from a lack of water. Water does seem such a plain and reasonable requirement that only some fatal intention would allow it to be denied.

Lying still and heavier than he has ever been, the boy recoils very slightly within his unfamiliar pyjamas. He believes, almost at once, that these are the clothes of some previous small patient who has died while on the ward, belongings left behind for the benefit of others and no further trace remaining. There are numerous, uncountably numerous, places where the boy's skin is being touched by the deadboy cloth. The jacket cuffs nuzzle limply against his wrists. It is very likely his arse is where a deadboy's arse has been and moreover his personal parts, which are meant to be secret, are maybe just comfortably settled in these trousers, because this is how the deadboy's used to rest. A coldandsmoky rush seems to rummage across him as he considers this and his left hand sneaks beneath the covers to make sure of himself and feel that all is well.

The hand seems slower and more clever than it used to be.

'Nurse ?' The boy tries his own mouth with the word and it emerges much as he'd expected.

'Yes.' She has paused because he has spoken and this makes him proud, but wary of coming responsibilities. 'Yes, what do you want ?'

'Can I have a glass of water?' He isn't thirsty, only curious.

'Yes.'

And the water is brought to him, shining with guilt, and set between his palms when he has raised himself through a wavering and thickened space. The boy holds his drink with monumental care – has to concentrate on gripping, as if he might soon forget how. He clings to its smoothness, to someone else's want, swallows loudly and with a kind of grin.

'Why does my head hurt?' Because it does – the left side of his skull and even his cheek are singing with a weird, dark ache, something exhilarating.

'A horse trod on you.'

This seems not unlikely.

He tucks the water inside himself, understands it is coiled now in a blue shape that perhaps half-fills him. 'Thank you.' He is polite. His father and mother would expect that of him. Then he slides back down to be flat, the water lapping and giggling as he moves.

A horse.

Yes.

There were horses.

There were lessons with horses to make the boy confident and able to sit up straight, a commanding presence in later life. A premeditated Christmas present that had started in January: ten o'clock on Saturday mornings, an hour with himself and various older, wilier boys in a wide, high barn – peaty and sawdusty stuff underfoot and everywhere alive with a humid and dangerous reek. Snow beyond the walls, but the boy hot, the boy feverish with horses.

They were large in the manner of trees – a threat of falling about them, of terrible damages waiting in the hollowsounding jaws and the long bones of their faces, the fierce, unsettled gouging of their hooves. They were big machinery with sudden blares of thinking, eyes that could not be relied upon. Hoisted and struggled up onto the leathercreak and sway of their backs the boy was too astonished to recall what he ought to do with his hands, his heels, his spine, his legs, his courage and his common sense. These were things that he could not learn, that he lost in the massive breathing of every animal.

At eleven fifteen on Saturday mornings he would sit in the back of his parents' car and he would smell of harness and terror. He would experimentally consider that his pain tomorrow might be easier if he had been beaten, that his bruises would be less shaming then.

No one has, in fact, beaten the boy at any time – although his mother did once hit him hard across the face and he does not know why. His father was already crying when this happened and the boy believes the crying was preemptively for him, his jolted mouth. The incident made him feel briefly and overly close to both his parents. Of course, he has often read stories where English boys are *flogged* in vast and incomprehensible schools and there are no parents – he sees it as wicked that he treasures these scenarios, prefers them to his current reality.

The boy holds thoughts he cannot name, he hates and wants and wants and hates his endless failures and the yelling instructor in the barn and the better riders' indolent disgust. On the drives home his personal parts, which are meant to be secret, will occasionally flinch and tease and he will form blurred wishes to be altered, simplified, cleaned.

When his mother and father ask him if he enjoys his riding lessons, he tells them, 'Yes.'

Although today – yesterday – the boy is pleasantly unsure of when – he was saved from having to tell his parents anything.

This is how you get to be alone in hospital.

A horse.

It was called Cobble and had a white nose and was in a bad temper. That morning they were strung and circled outside in a field – no more barn because this was meant to be the spring – but the ground was stiff again, ice layers cracking over empty ruts and slush where the sunlight was lying. Cobble didn't like the cold. Cobble strayed and headshook and his mind turned, the boy could taste it, a slithery panic before the hooves ever dug, or the charge ever started, the bolt.

No one had told the boy how to stop a bolting horse.

Some shouting somebody loomed alongside him, reaching for the reins, but this drove Cobble faster and out onto tarmac, out to a road, out into a blindwhite pitching sky, flogged breath, clinging, sweating and the small decision, and then much larger, that the boy should let go, must be over with this and drop.

Head injury.

In what is still the boy's favourite story a man fell from a ladder and was given a head injury and when he woke he could see to the future and find the lost.

This made him famous.

He was called Peter.

Which is the boy's name.

Head injury.

The man was Dutch – being from Holland means you're Dutch. Which is confusing.

Dutch sounds like Scotch, but Scotch is a drink and Scottish is a person, so the boy is not Scotch – the boy's mother and father are quite sure about that.

If he says he is Scotch he will be wrong.

If he laughs too outloud he will be wrong.

If he spoons his soup towards himself he will be wrong.

It would be equally wrong for the boy to keep a hard light of intention burning at his heart, a need to draw in calamity and blows to the brain.

He does it anyway.

And now he has one, a head injury, he holds it like a smile poured in under his hair.

The boy pictures his brain as newly alert and changed to a glistening mass, a larger cousin of the oyster his grandfather made him eat last summer – told him it was living, that it would forage and thrive beneath his skin and scour him out into a better health. He is sure the accident has roused his oystermind and that it is currently flexing, searching forward with an appetite he admires. He hopes it has decided to look at his future.

The effort of this will surely be taxing and the boy is not alarmed when it presses his eyelids unstoppably shut and sets the night running and swinging and plunging him to sleep. He leaves himself and travels.

But it is, quite naturally, his past which takes him, rides him, makes the boy a creature of belief – he has no other possibilities. So into a song he goes, into the other time he saw his father cry – head back and the words there, red and wet in his daddy's mouth and at the end of them weeping. The boy's happiness, he dreams, will be in evenings where he sings and there are men about him and hugs which cuff his head and magnificent griefs, such marvellous injuries to shape him and let him rage.

His mother's table, on which he must never lean his elbows during meals, shines oddly and draws his attention to stand beside it and peer down. Laid along the mahogany, he sees his older body, naked and washed. The boy studies his wish to be solid, short-bearded, complete, and to have impressive arms with one tattoo – a little flag with writing underneath it which he cannot read, but realises is important. His personal parts, which are meant to be secret, remain as he knows them and are then transparent and then, after that, are spilled away. Their loss seems justified, a proper punishment for spoiling the table's shine. It is by no means extraordinary that he feels them more than ever when they are gone.

And at around this time, two men who are foreign come to resurrect him – the boy has been told about resurrection and also resurrectionists and both these things excite him. As his limbs shiver and tick, the men open his body like a book and dig into the truth of him, wrist deep, and find a metal fish, a rifle and a chanter, the shine of a plough, forgetfulness twice-distilled, broom flowers and roses, a lobster upended and balanced on its claws, a woman's hair dragged from its scalp and thick as jute, a righteous and clever tawse, a burning rivet and a burning brand and a burning cross and a burning word, a collar the colour of blood, a whale bone carved with a ship and on the ship a man who travels, who will scour the world, who will march in a black line and clean it, burn it, bleed it and suffer as he steps and held in his hand is a heart, a sleeping heart, a hunted heart, a heart like a dirty hole through to nowhere that he lifts above his head.

He waves to the boy and the boy waves back.

This waving troubles the boy – it grips him.

'Hold still.'

He is seasick as he rises up into the ward, hears the tiny panting of the pressure-cuff as it inflates. His arm is stinging and it frightens him.

'I said hold still. You can be brave, can't you?' The nurse, another nurse, whispering. 'Can't you try and be brave?'

This will be a predictable element of his recovery. Every three hours, night and day, someone will come to measure the condition of his blood, put the chill of a thermometer under his tongue.

'Don't bite it.'

For the boy this will be wearying and unheroic.

Tomorrow afternoon his mother will arrive and sit next to his bed with a new copy of *The Beano* and *The Dandy* and, in a paper bag, the *Oor Wullie* annual he was not allowed for Christmas, because it is full of rough talk and ways that nobody decent should behave. His father will not visit, but will sit in the parked car outside and listen to football reports on the radio – this will be because the smell of hospitals makes him sick. He will send his best. If he knew about the *Oor Wullie* annual he would probably not.

The boy will take his comics and his mother's kiss on his forehead and on the one of his cheeks which is nearest to her. He will think he doesn't want to read them, because he suspects reading might be difficult, but he won't say that, for fear of being rude. He will not know what to do when he sees that she is very sad about him and so he will pretend that his head hurts more than it does and she will nod a lot and put a bottle of Lucozade wrapped in crinkling yellowstuff on the bedside cabinet which is his while he is here and then she will stand up and he will suddenly regret that she is leaving.

Once he is alone he will still have the scent of her on his skin. There will be an afternoon in thirty years time when he will be caught by that exact perfume as he walks behind a woman in the street and he will follow her and want to touch her shoulder and to scream and to be hurt by strangers until he cannot think.

But while he is a boy in his bed at the edge of that first morning after it happened he is brilliant with wishes, unsteadied by so many opening paths towards whoever he may be. His powers, he believes, will be remarkable.

If the boy truly could see the rest of his oncoming life, he would appreciate this is the kindest way in which he will ever be wrong. This is the best.

ALAN WARNER

Born in 1964, Alan Warner was raised in the Scottish port town of Oban; he now lives in County Wicklow, dividing his time between Ireland, Scotland and Spain. He is the author of five novels: *Morvern Callar* (1995) – which won the Somerset Maugham Award; *These Demented Lands* (1997) – an Encore Award-winner; *The Sopranos* (1998) – Saltire Society Scottish Book of the Year Award; *The Man Who Walks* (2002) – Saltire Society Award short-listed; and *The Worms Can Carry Me to Heaven* (2006). His next novel, *The Stars in the Bright Sky*, will be published in May 2010. He also writes short stories including, for example, *After the Vision*, which features in *Children of Albion Rovers: An Antholgy of New Scottish Writing* (1996).

Warner's critically lauded debut novel was made into a feature film of the same name – released in 2002, directed by Lynne Ramsay and starring Samantha Morton, the film, too, was well-received.

Alan Warner

In 2003, Warner was nominated one of *Granta*'s Best Young British Novelists and *Scotland on Sunday* has praised the 'bold statement of intent . . .' in the author's work ' . . .different from much Scottish fiction in its audacious rejection of realism, maleness and the urban landscape'.

BLIND BILLY'S PRIDE

Alan Warner

In the early 1970s when I was still editor of our little town newspaper, the *Port Star*, it was the old siren of the fire station which signalled the start of every gala day raft and swim race.

On the low-tide shore, by the pier, the whole town would line the sea wall railings and a disorganised plunge of hearty swimmers tiptoed or stumbled, fell or ran over the shingle and seaweed into the printing-ink black water of the bay. Before the siren had died off, the sponsored rafts also kicked away from the pier struts and began rowing. A sort of debased Venetian carnival began. Each raft has a sponsor or theme: Vikings, nuclear submarine, the car-shaped MacKinnon's Garage, Saint Columba with an entourage from the hairdresser of sculling young nuns in blue eye shadow, or one year a belligerent GIs-in-Vietnam raft; a porcupine of harpoon guns – which was all the police would allow them – though Dochie Docherty still managed to send off a dart, like a flare, high to the south.

Catcalls faded as the rafts beat out towards the warning pole on Shelter Island's shore. Bobbing heads of sedate breaststrokers and sawing arms of the crawlers frothed towards the tilted mast of a sunk wreck in the boatyard which they must circle, without touching, before heading back.

The gala day issue was always a big seller of the *Port Star* for us – as big as cattle-market specials, or the Christmas edition. Our editorial office in those manual typewriter days was small and the newspaper still printed on premises by the compositor and his sixteen year-old son, down on the ground floor. 'Shutters' Stuart, our chief photographer (our only photographer) was a big part of what you could call smooth running at the *Port Star*. I would often encourage Stuart to pen his own features to go with his photographs. Who in our town can forget Stuart's close-up of Whiskers Lennon with the singed eyebrows, the once-abundant nostril-hair melted? The bold black headline above: **Beware the Dangers of Slurry-spreading**.

Whiskers had been towing a powerful new slurry spreader behind his tractor but too near an electricity pylon. The flying, wet cow-muck touched the high-tension wire, made a connection and the high voltage flowed down the thrown stream, through the farm equipment and farmer. Whiskers said, up in the cab, he could see his own skeleton so clearly that he distinguished dark arthritis areas in his wrist and fingers. He claimed it would save him another visit to the hospital for an X-ray.

That gala day of 1973, as the rafts rounded the mast and the strongest swimmers arrived back in, ducking their bodies for standing depth, 'Shutters' Stuart was in position on the slipway as per usual, looking for good shots of faces-about-town. Predictably, first out the waters came both the competitive, muscled, high-school PE teachers. To be polite, Stuart held up his old Leica, pretending to take a snap of them. Others emerged: dripping hugely from the brine came Big Nanna's beaming red face, so familiar to us from behind the counter at Liptons. Not so photogenic.

Last swimmer out – he swam every year – was old Blind Billy Paterson, nearly sixty-five years of age and sightless since birth, beloved by all the town and navigated across the waters by the healthy shouts of his fellow swimmers. 'This way Billy; don't bump the ferry.'

He got his usual round of applause. We had used Blind Billy's photo three years before and maybe could get away with using his image once more. His sister, Donna – no spring chicken herself – quickly stepped forward, fussed around his bandy legs with a towel and helped him up the shingle. Otherwise it was pretty mean pickings for photos that year. There were no dramatic sinkings, nor raised oars of anger between pirates and Lord Nelson. As every year, the police raft with its ironic, spinning blue light came in second to the lifeboat crew.

The crowd dispersed to see colourful floats convoy down the main street – including, on the back of the Alexanders' coal lorry, a disgracefully loud, long-haired rock band called the *Psychedelic Pixies* who threw out 2,000 Gestetner-turned leaflets which blew up and down our pavements for a week. Each leaflet read: *The Psychedelic Pixies Say Keep Scotland Tidy*.

Publishing day – Thursday morning – came the phone call. My wife sat up suddenly in bed beside me.

'Oh my goodness. What an hour.' It was half past seven.

Stuart's voice said, 'Get your breeks on.'

'What is it?'

'If the garages have the bales delivered, pick them up and bring them back here right now. If they won't give them to you, buy the lot.'

'What's wrong?'

'We're going to have to recall the paper.'

'Recall it! How much is out?'

'Most of the town.'

'Give us a clue, Stuart.'

'Easier if you just see.'

Towards the newspaper office, I drove my Hillman Imp beyond the speed limit. A newsworthy event in itself. I presumed our mistake must have been a terrible, socially awkward mistaken identity in the pages, but I could not fathom what could be so serious? Everybody knows one another in our small port town, so mistaken identity is almost an impossibility. The only fertile ground for mistaken identity, was our annual *Port Star* bonniest baby photo competition. On one occasion, Ian Fung, aged three months – son of the charming proprietor of our only Chinese restaurant took on a distinctly occidental appearance. While in the adjacent photograph, the three month-old son of Mrs Nicolson, chief organiser of tea evenings up at Episcopalian Hall, took on an undeniable Oriental look, which gave her recent and well-featured missionary visit to Hong Kong a deeply unfortunate undertone. But there was no baby competition in this issue.

When I parked at our offices, the driver from National Carriers was sitting in his yellow cab, smoking and shrugging. Stuart had the printer and his son – who was visibly sneering – stacking up bales of newspapers awaiting shipment, well back from the dispatch door. I dragged a paper from the top of a bale, tearing it. Bottom of the page was the gala day swim feature. I could see Stuart had chosen a photo of a broadly smiling Blind Billy stood in the surf. Then I looked a little further down.

Blind Billy Paterson was emerging from the waters, shaking his withered chin flap, his sightless gaze canted slightly up, towards our glum skies. Billy, as always, was wearing a swim cap and that black, one-piece gentleman's swim costume – like something from before the war, in the days of bathing huts. But on the crotch area of the slightly slack costume, it had very clearly come free from the enclosing fabric and it hung, in full visibility. How could it not hang.

'Oh no!'

'I only looked at the negative on the light box then passed it to print.' Stuart shook his head. 'How did I miss yon thing? And him a bachelor.'

We managed to have all ferry shipments over to the islands returned to the office and so isolated the immediate disgrace to the mainland alone. Editions did not depart on the 0740 train for Glasgow. We caught the early delivery van to the outlying villages by a phone call to Fiona Millan who we all knew fine was seeing that van driver and he, anxious to reach Fiona early since her husband came home for lunch, only dropped off bales on the way back. Postal subscriptions had not gone out either, so Blind Billy's shame did not travel to Nova Scotia – nor even, where a single subscription travelled weekly – was far Japan ever to witness it.

However, editions had reached all the shops and both supermarkets of our town. They say in this place that if a rumour starts on the top floor it has reached the street before the contents of a flushed lavatory. Blind Billy's front page edition of our *Port Star* sold out in hours, breaking all records. Our pleading fell on unsympathetic shopkeepers who wanted another print run and asked if this idea might become a weekly feature. Opposite the Catholic girls' school, demand was so high an excitable, uniformed queue stretched across the forecourt for the wee petrol station shop. Teachers had sixth-year pupils bringing them back an extra copy. I learned two nuns from the retreat above town, suddenly emerged with a suspicious enthusiasm for that week's latest local news.

Blind Billy and his sister lived in the bottom half of a small villa at the upper end of High Street. Blind Billy had been dispatched to his den – the garden shed, where daily he assiduously scanned the airwaves and especially the *Shipping Forecast* on a big wireless. I observed the house's interior: Billy's white canes in the umbrella stand of the porch, glass-bowl lamps on chains, frilly antimacassars, metallic wallpaper; a paper doily gentility to soften the hard edges of Donna's responsibilities and spinster existence.

The talk was polite and overwhelmed with euphemisms.

She said, 'He knows nothing but what about when he finds out?'

I replied, 'Miss Paterson. What matters is that someone who is not hurt yet will always remain unhurt.'

'In this town of sinners?' she shook her head definitely.

'Billy can't read the newspaper. And since I'm responsible I'll use it as the antidote.'

Old Peter Scarley, my journalism teacher in Birmingham always told me to 'get their attention and shake 'em by the lapels'. I printed it, not prominently but on the bottom of the front page the following Thursday:

'And the cock crew twice.'

I knew I had their attention.

I wrote:

Can this proud town keep silent? It is only one set of ears which matter and we must protect the ears of one unfortunate among us. ('Not unfortunate in every way!' I know the men shouted across, in the pubs).

My challenge to my own town finished in stentorian tones:

Peter denied Jesus three times before the cock crew twice. Let us all, not for one thoughtless moment, deny our responsibility to another.'

Obscure I know, but with a hint of grandeur; and the mix of crossword clue with religiosity was suitably threatening.

I was sure I noticed subtle changes in the timbre of our town. People seemed to move with a new enthusiasm and sense of mission on our wet streets. I was greeted with knowing smiles. In solidarity we all feared those few words, hovering like angry wasps around Blind Billy and words alone endangered him. But words were never spoken about the newspaper photograph near him. School children continued to assist Blind Billy to cross the road in those days before audible pedestrian crossings. I saw fearsome battleaxes from the Women's Association happily greet him and crowd around to shake hands with Billy and his smiling sister on the esplanade. I saw afternoon drunks place an arm gently on Billy's shoulders. Yes, I saw smiles, I saw knowing glances in our ugly, sighted world, but what I never heard was a single utterance. In Billy's realm of sounds, all was in its usual order. Perhaps my townsfolk were cheered to find, how can I put it: potential vitality hidden in unlikely places?

A year went by and Billy swam the gala once more. Proof that he had not been informed. The town breathed a collective sigh of relief as it noted the new, well-knotted, modern swimming trunks.

Billy received an ovation as he beached. It was his last gala swim before he retreated to calm and measured lengths of our town's new, indoor heated swimming pool, one evening a week.

I have been called the conscience of this town on more than one occasion. But really, I leave such distinctions to Father Ardlui, in the confessionals of the cathedral or to Glasgow Glen, our CID man and his grim escorting south, of various individuals.

Blind Billy passed away and went up to swim with the Old Dodger in the sky at least a decade ago. Standing at the back, I attended his funeral. Who didn't? The whole town was there. He had more of a turn-out than I shall have.

Two generations have now forgotten Blind Billy's shame – what should really be called Blind Billy's pride. Nobody knows, cares or gossips about it now. This town is full of youngsters wearing earphones. I don't know if they are listening to telephones or to music; there are newcomers emerging from sports cars but dressed like ghillies. Perhaps no one remembers?

I still pass old Donna Paterson on the street today or in the new superstore and we nod to each other, politely. Sometimes I wonder if it all happened but I know many will have the proof: brittle newspaper cuttings, scissored out, folded somewhere in the back of desk drawers or up on bookshelves inside a hardback which smells of the past. Proof that a whole town can keep a literal silence for good reasons – not just for bad.

ACKNOWLEDGEMENTS

Ali Smith's 'Common' first appeared in the *Sunday Times Magazine*, 19 April 2009. Andrew O'Hagan's 'Foreigners' first appeared in *The New Yorker*, 6 December 2004. Reproduced with thanks.

There are a number of people without whose help, encouragement and generosity this project would not have been possible. I would like to thank particularly Bob McDevitt and Wendy McCance at Hachette Scotland; Gavin Wallace at the Scottish Arts Council; Marc Lambert at the Scottish Book Trust; Robyn Marsack, Lilias Fraser and Peggy Hughes at the Scottish Poetry Library; Carolyn Rae at the Scottish Government Communications Office and Catherine Lockerbie and Roland Gulliver at the Edinburgh International Book Festival. At *Scotland on Sunday*, both the current and previous editors, Ian Stewart and Les Snowdon, were firm supporters of this idea from its inception, and special thanks as well go to the Deputy Editor, Kenny Farquharson, Fiona Leith, the Review Editor, Jenny McNeely from the Library and Alan Macdonald, Pictures Editor. My personal thanks to my wife, Sam Kelly, who cast her exceptional editorial eye over the manuscript. Above all, thanks to the authors who so intelligently and productively responded to the brief.